TWENTY-FIRST CENTURY TEACHING GUIDE FOR INDIAN SCHOOLS

SCIENCE BOOK II

Tania Ghosh is a highly experienced educator, author, and curriculum innovator with over a decade of experience teaching physics at the IBDP, IGCSE, and A Level programmes. She holds an M.Sc. in Physics and is currently a high school physics teacher at Modern High School International, Kolkata, where she also serves as an ATL team member. Tania is the founder of FutureEd Curriculum Designs, a global community for educators, and a contributor to the IB Exchange Physics Development Team. She has also served as an ATL Coordinator at Calcutta International School. A doctoral candidate in Curriculum and Instruction, she holds numerous advanced certifications from prestigious institutions such as Harvard, MIT, and Cambridge. Her mission is to empower students and educators by creating engaging, future-ready learning experiences that foster lifelong curiosity.

AF528174

PEDAGOGY SERIES

Twenty-First Century

TEACHING GUIDE FOR INDIAN SCHOOLS

Science 2

Tania Ghosh

For Classes 6–8

hachette INDIA

First published in 2025 by Hachette India
(Registered name: Hachette Book Publishing India Pvt. Ltd)
An Hachette UK company
www.hachetteindia.com

1

Text copyright © 2025 Hachette India

All rights reserved. No part of the publication may be reproduced, stored in a retrieval system (including but not limited to computers, disks, external drives, electronic or digital devices, e-readers, websites), or transmitted in any form or by any means (including but not limited to cyclostyling, photocopying, docutech or other reprographic reproductions, mechanical, recording, electronic, digital versions) without the prior written permission of the publisher, nor be otherwise circulated in any form of binding or cover other than that in which it is published and without a similar condition being imposed on the subsequent purchaser.

All content and facts within the book have been updated and verified to the best extent possible. Any inadvertent omissions brought to our attention in writing will be remedied in future editions.

Images and URLs used in the book have been taken from Shutterstock.com and Wikipedia Commons, accessed in September 2025. QR codes, if any, included in the book lead to video links which belong to the respective channels/video platforms that have posted them.

Subsequent edition/reprint specifications may be subject to change, including but not limited to cover or inside finishes, paper, text colour, and/or colour sections.

ISBN: 978-93-5731-421-3

Hachette Book Publishing India Pvt. Ltd
4th & 5th Floors, Corporate Centre,
Plot No. 94, Sector 44, Gurugram 122003, India

Typeset in Adobe Garamond Pro 11.5/16
by Content Respondus
New Delhi

MIX
Paper | Supporting responsible forestry
FSC® C010615

Printed and bound in India
by Thomson Press India Ltd.

Contents

Preface vii

1. Sherlock Holmes Knew Piaget 1
2. Vygotsky 20
3. Sociocultural Integration 41
4. Maslow 65
5. Gardner 81
6. Science Through the Arts 94
7. Kolb 104
8. Abstract Conceptualization 111
9. Skinner 122
10. ADDIE Model 148

Image Copyright Information 167

Preface

As a student I was never fond of examinations. It felt like a chore to me. Yet when it was interaction in the classroom or a challenge given by teachers, the love of discovering new knowledge always kept me going.

In my teaching practices I have tried to give more importance to concepts than content. The beauty of co-creating knowledge together with students has inspired me to experiment with different types of pedagogical practices.

This book began as a series of discussions of different ways of engaging students in a classroom. All my colleagues, mentors and my educator family at FutureEd Curriculum Designs have enriched my thoughts and ideas of teaching throughout the years of my educator journey.

The NEP has outlined the ways by which teachers can focus on concepts and skills while delivering lessons. This book aids teachers with the ideas of educational theory and theorists, and bridges it with varied teaching strategies that align with it. These teaching strategies are steeped into all the skills that the NEP focuses on.

The focus has been to incorporate the topics that are mapped in the CBSE Science curriculum. This should help teachers of the national curriculum to have an understanding of how to use the book in planning classroom strategies that engage students and help the teaching learning process.

I am deeply grateful to my publishers for this opportunity that has made me delve into pedagogical practices further. The stupendous learning over the last few months was exhaustive and enriching.

Here is to more discoveries and learning! I hope you learn or relearn some aspects of varied teaching practices spelt out in the book.

Chapter 1

Sherlock Holmes Knew Piaget

Are you shocked?

He did not know John Piaget!

It is only my mind building hypothetical connections.

The reason why I speculated this was because of the way Sherlock Holmes approached the case of "The Adventure of the Speckled Band". The cognitive process employed by Holmes aligned with the Piagetian concepts of development and learning.

The process of problem-solving starts from abstract thinking, forming a hypothesis to systematic problem-solving linked with the study established by Piaget. Holmes gathers clues, forms hypotheses, carefully observes, and tests his hypotheses.

Holmes behaves like a learner as per Piaget's educational perspective – assimilating new information and accommodating new mental models to fit data.

The balance between assimilation and accommodation is the foundation of Piaget's idea of learning through discovery: interaction and exploration rather than passive reception of facts.

- Challenging the existing understandings while stimulating cognitive growth
- Promoting logical reasoning
- Critiquing concepts that are irrelevant

Social interaction also takes shape in this story via his collaboration with Watson. Watson is his go-to person when Holmes needs to refine and articulate his reasoning.

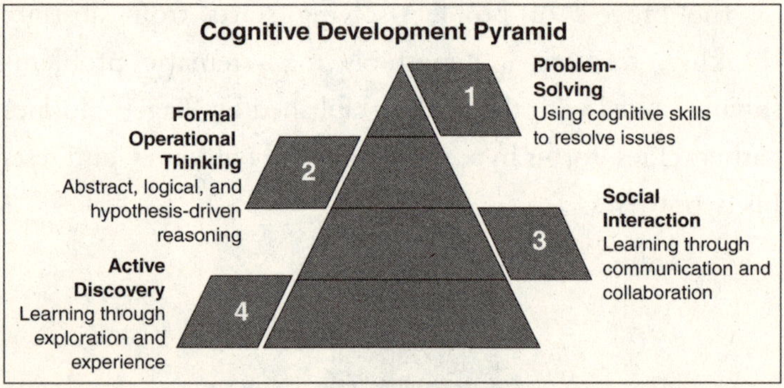

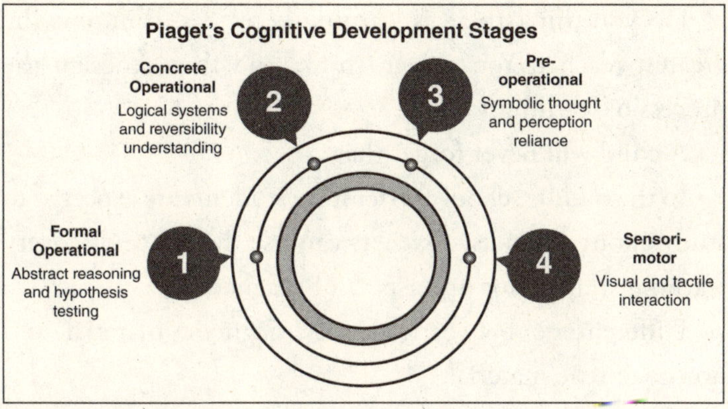

Teaching-Learning Strategies of Piaget in Middle School Science

Active Discovery Learning

Back in the early 2000s, in the wake of globalization, there were so many things that came to our grocery shops. One such was kernels of corn in packets that would pop into popcorn.

Jaw-dropping, eye-widening experience – popcorn at home!

My friends and I had a plan. We tried the trick at home. We got some corn cobs, cut off the kernels with a knife, put them into butter, and covered them… waiting for them to pop.

No! They did not.

Were we afraid of failure? No! We laughed and joked about it. Though we did not discover how to pop the corn successfully, we understood how to not!

Do you think there is learning here? Yes! Failure is the greatest teacher. You reflect, think, and then redesign the process of learning.

A child will never forget that.

In the middle school curriculum, students are expected to study about magnets. Teachers can use the active discovery learning strategy for one aspect of magnetism:

Differentiate between magnet/magnetic material and non-magnetic material.

Keep the activity open-ended.

Instruments to be used: A magnet, a magnetic material, and a non-magnetic material. Additionally, you need a bar magnet.

Students are going to interact with the materials and discuss. They will be given a worksheet that looks like this:

You have been given a few objects. **List them here:** **1.** **2.** **3.** **4.**
You have to determine… **1. Which one is a magnet? Write down how you determined it.** ____________________________

2. **Which one is not a magnet? Write down how you determined it.**

---

3. **Which one is a magnetic material? Write down how you determined it.**

Providing Concrete Experiences Before Abstract Concepts

Night and day…How many of you remember that geography class where you actually understood how day and night work.

The torch on one side, the ball rotating on the other side. That is when the strength of demonstration opens up the understanding of a concept – why day and night happen.

The demonstration acts as a concrete experience, where the student sees how the side toward the light experiences day and the other side is in darkness. The student understands the how and why of things.

A similar concept is the concept of "fields" in magnetism. Students will play with magnets, understand how they work, experiment with them, and give you answers relating to experiments. When it comes to understanding the magnetic field, it becomes an extremely abstract concept. Something that they cannot see, touch, or hear falls on deaf ears. They learn it by heart just to pass.

When critical questions on the same are asked, they are clueless. We do not require students who will not be able to engage in looking at solutions to novel problems in the future.

The linking of concrete with abstract and building the bridge in between is what we are looking at.

This is what teachers can do:

1. **Introduce the concept in class:** How a magnet's force works. How force has an area of influence. "I am talking to you in the class – you can hear me; can a person one kilometer away hear me? This classroom is being influenced by my voice – you are hearing my voice, hopefully listening to it too."
   This area of influence can be shown using lines of force. We don't see it, but it is there. Our eyes don't have the capability to see the lines of force, but let us see what we can do.

The teacher can use iron filings on a firm piece of paper and one or two magnets underneath it. Arrange the magnet underneath the paper and sprinkle the filings. Tap on the paper.

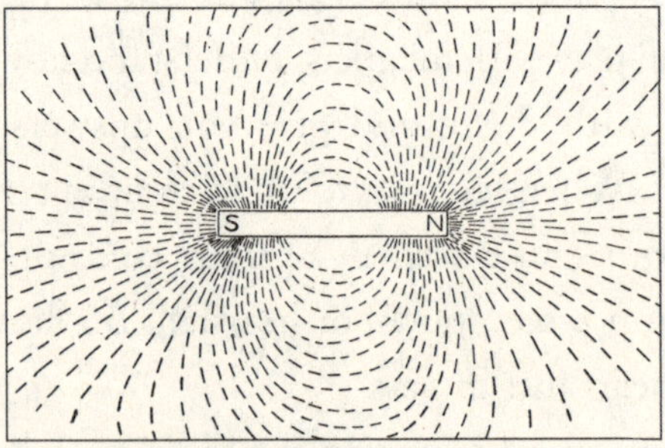

Force fields and lines of force

Explain what they are seeing here. Ask them to relate to dense and sparse regions of the iron filings. Connect the idea of force fields and distance to consolidate.

Here, teaching begins with tangible hands-on experiences, observing phenomena and connecting with abstract concepts of force fields.

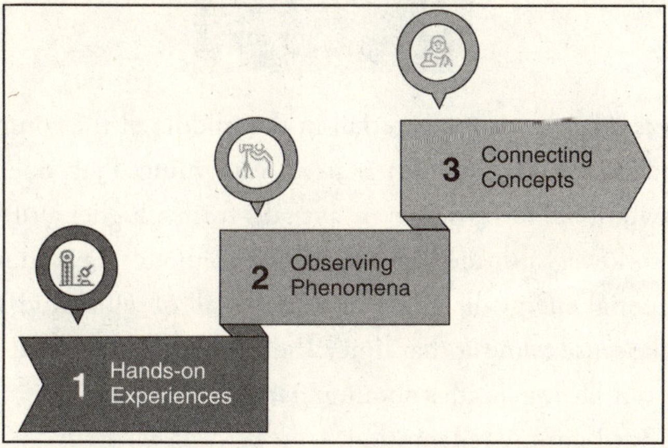

Cognitive Conflict and Equilibration

The story of Newton and the apple falling is known to all. Once upon a time, there was a curious boy named Newton. He was sitting under a tree, and an apple fell from it. Now, most of us would wipe it and eat it. He, however, started thinking about why the apple fell. Voila! After a lot of back and forth with math, the idea of gravity was born.

I was once visiting a waterfall in the middle of the country (India), and my cousin started explaining that due to gravitational force, water always falls from a higher altitude to a lower altitude. He also talked about gravitational potential energy, height, and velocity, all of which did not make sense to me at that time. The smarty-pants bugged me for not having an idea about *gravity*!

But I got my redemption.

Let me share how. I will tell you exactly what my teacher did. It was called "capillary action in plants".

She got a stalk of leaves and put them in a transparent jar that had potassium permanganate solution. She did this in the morning. When we were packing up to go home, we saw purple streaks along the stalk, almost reaching up to the leaves.

What was happening? The liquid was moving up?

The teacher nodded in agreement.

I came back and showed off my knowledge of "capillary action".

Let's see how we can intentionally teach this to our students.

Create Cognitive Conflict Situations

The teacher can talk about the properties of water, as shown in the following picture. Or ask: Tell me in which direction the water is flowing in this waterfall.

Iguazu Falls

The students will definitely answer that it is flowing down from a higher to a lower altitude.

Challenge their existing understanding.

Does water always flow from higher to lower altitudes? Are you sure?

No! Not always!

Some students will oppose this: "No, ma'am. How can you say so? Water always from higher to lower altitude because of gravity."

Show them the following news article:

> **September 21:** More than ten years ago, reports swept through India that the elephant-headed Hindu deity, Lord Ganesha, was miraculously drinking milk from a spoon. The story spread across the world with remarkable speed, drawing comparisons to wildfire. From city streets to remote villages, people carried spoons of milk to Ganesha idols, watching in awe as the liquid seemed to vanish. "Ganpati is drinking milk," echoed through the lanes and marketplaces that day.
>
> The phenomenon drew massive crowds, with long lines forming outside temples as millions sought to witness or participate in the offering. Within a week, questions began to emerge. Was this truly a divine act that enabled the idols to consume milk, or was it the deep faith of devotees that made them believe it so? The article that follows explores the science and reasoning behind the celebrated moment when Hindu idols appeared to sip milk from their followers.

Thousands of people around the country lined up for hours to experience this "miracle". Could an idol really sip milk? The liquid was moving the opposite way (upwards).

A disequilibrium sets in. Students try to make sense of it. You see a lot of chatter. Let them talk among themselves. Let them suggest a reason, no matter how ridiculous it is.

They mostly will not have heard about capillary action. This motivates students to go back home and research. Ask them to come back with a small write-up on what they could research. Stick these pages (preferably chits) on the noticeboard for all to see.

From the chits, draw out the reasoning with student consensus. Then establish the learning objective that includes ideas of capillary action in plants.

Start your lesson with a happy mind, knowing that your lesson will be a breeze. A deeper conceptual growth is guaranteed.

Scaffolded Learning and Guided Discovery

What fun those treasure-hunt games were! I am sure your students also get excited at the prospect of participating in a treasure hunt. What do you think it does to the psyche of a child that they get so excited about it?

It is human. Whenever a child is cognitively challenged, it is inherent human nature to seek out the end. The euphoria of finding the answer to a question has been stymied by the "information-giver"; in other words, the traditional teacher. Think about getting information after information and being asked to put it into practice.

Where is the fun in that?

If you can playfully challenge and guide a child to seek knowledge, they are invested in it just to validate the fact that they are capable of it. This gives a huge boost to the confidence of an individual. Think of puzzles, Sudoku, and crosswords. These have stood the test of time in keeping the general populace engaged because they give people a sense of achievement.

It takes time, it does, to ideate, plan, and execute such an impactful experience. But can you not try it once in a while?

Let's take the idea of how the electric bell works. Instead of the teacher telling the students – SCAFFOLD – print a picture of the electric bell and erase the labels. Maybe draw dialog boxes in place of the labels. Ask them to identify the parts. Direct with numbered arrows and ask them to build a story around the arrows – answering the why, how, and what questions.

Of course, they should first make the commentary stick to the logic. Then provide a flowchart with a fixed number of boxes. A rough plan is shown below:

Appropriate materials	Picture of an electromagnet Worksheet	The teacher may put up an unlabeled picture of an electric bell or put it up on a screen. Draw arrows for the commentary sequence. Keep flowchart boxes as a worksheet.
Ask probing questions.	Keep pointing to the arrow that you are referring to.	Teacher asks: Can you spot the coils of the electromagnet? Write a function of an electromagnet. Can you see an iron strip?
Facilitate discussions.	Keep asking different students. Use random names from your class register to ask questions, or you can use the "catch the ball and answer" strategy. It is best to avoid the "put your hands up if you know the answer" strategy.	What do you think will happen when the electromagnet is switched on? What do you think is the function of the gong? The iron strip goes back to its original position. Why does that happen?

Help students construct knowledge actively.	At the end, the teacher writes the steps for the students to check. Ask them to see whether what they have written includes all the points.	The teacher may go around to ensure that the students have done self-correction on the flowchart.

Peer Interaction and Group Learning

My teaching career has been a long and fruitful one. Two highlights have been my colleagues and my students. I have learned equally from both. I cannot stress enough how the process of a school functioning was explained to me, not by lecture but by sheer observation. What was to be done was not explicitly told to me, but I was given the liberty to choose which avenue I wanted to go along.

During these years, I also changed jobs. Every time, there was a colleague who broke the ice, helped me ease in, and explained things that were new to me. It was a whole lot better than if an instructional manual had simply been handed to me.

Social interaction in a formal setting helps professionals learn better. Imagine how it could help your students.

How would you know that there is a scarcity of water, and how d0oes it affect life?

Divide the class into two groups; these are presented with two different scenarios.

Scenario 1: Water abundance in a region

Average daily use per person: 142-154 liters (e.g., Singapore)

Divide the daily needs:

- Washroom
- Kitchen (with cooking)
- Household
- Drinking

Scenario 2: Water scarcity in a region

Average daily use per person: 10-20 liters (e.g., Singapore)

Divide the daily needs:

- Washroom
- Kitchen (with cooking)
- Household
- Drinking

This leads to a lot of things: cooperative problem-solving, dealing with peer conflict, exposing them to different viewpoints, etc. This helps them in cognitive development and understanding.

They have to be asked about the reasoning and how they think people in areas of water scarcity manage. Students immediately appreciate and empathize with the situation all around the world.

Differentiated Instruction Based on Developmental Readiness

So, this happened just last year. A student who seemed to be very inattentive in class lost all his practice papers. This was something he had been doing for a long time – referring to the feedback. He was almost ready for the exam. Two days before the examination, he lost his bag, and his notebooks were all gone.

I managed to give him notes, but the practice papers, books… Provide a space after "…" I could not manage to provide those. I was quite nervous for him.

However, he came on the D-day, beaming. "Don't worry! I have seen it all on YouTube!"

I kept my fingers crossed. Though he could not achieve what he was intending to, all was not lost. He managed to get decent grades and I heaved a sigh of relief.

Different people can learn using different methods. It is not just in the classroom, or through books and notes, or by practicing Q&A. There could be so many differentiations that could be made for students with different learning traits.

The topic the teacher could choose is the water cycle – rain, thunder, lightning, evaporation. Students can be given formative tasks, allotting time for them to create artistic reflections and interpretations of lessons. Care should be taken that the task is such that it challenges students but does not overwhelm or frustrate them.

They can be asked to choose any one of the following:

- Look for videos on YouTube that explain the topics listed above.
- Use infographics that connect all these topics together.
- Provide an audio recording of the student who narrates the concepts together.

- Get students to act out a scene or skit with all the topics connected.
- Incorporate charts and illustrations to explain the topics.

What is essentially important is setting a common rubric and success criteria. An example is given below:

Type of Submission	Details (5 marks)	All Content Covered (5 marks)	Logical Scientific Concepts Tied Together (5 marks)	Clear Communication (5 marks)	Qualitative Feedback
Videos	Not more than four minutes				
Infographics	An A4 sheet/ one digital page				
Audio	Not more than four minutes				
Skit	Not more than five minutes				
Chart and illustrations	One chart				

Concrete operational students would focus on logical thinking with concrete objects. Formal operational students can work with scientific reasoning.

> In qualitative feedback, the teacher can mention the areas where the student could have improved. Always provide constructive feedback.
>
> "It was not up to the mark" is bad feedback.
>
> "The connection of the water cycle to thunder and lightning was not explained correctly" is constructive and workable feedback.

Encouraging Reflective Thinking and Metacognition

This is for all teachers who step out of their comfort zone. A big salute to you!

It requires a different type of courage to try something new in front of students. And believe me, most of the time, it does not go as planned.

Let me tell you about such an incident where my strategy did not hold water at all.

I was teaching middle school mathematics, and the topic was ratio and proportion. I thought, *Let's make it relevant.* It was the summer, and cold mocktails would be welcome by all. So, I took a bit of this and that and made simple mocktails. My purpose was for them to appreciate that the proportion of one liquid changes the taste of the entire mocktail.

But… all of them tried to come up to taste it. One could not be differentiated from the other. Chaos ensued. I had to stop.

I went back, feeling like a failure.

Did I forget about it?

No! I went back and rethought the whole thing. It was not structured; it had no quantifiable objectives to achieve. So… I turned it into a project with proper objectives, rubrics, things to be achieved, explanations to be given, and responsibilities. I took small steps, looked at logistics, and the project was done on a summer day; all of the school came down to have delicious, but each slightly different, mocktails.

A similar, slightly challenging activity would be a "thought composition". What is that?

Say you have been teaching students about shadows.

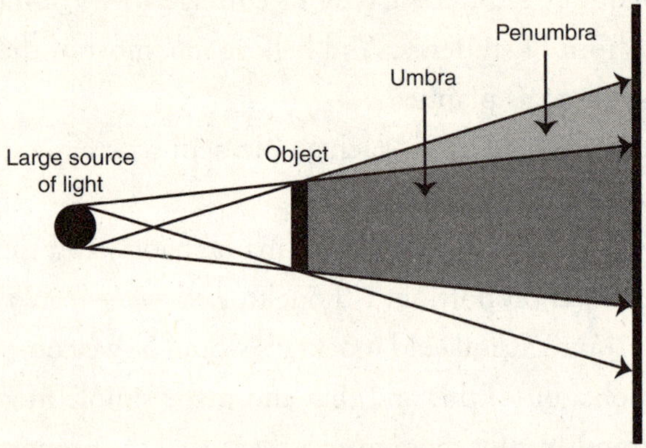

Students are asked to write an explanation of total and partial eclipses using the ideas of umbra and penumbra, with scaffolding questions. You can see whether they understand that the umbra is total and penumbra is partial.

Once that is done, we now come to the fun bit.

Write a thought composition on how weird the world would be if light did not travel in straight lines.

What are thought compositions?

In the sciences, they are concepts that are hypothetical in nature and cannot really be tested. What they do is cater to higher-order thinking skills that enable students to reflect on their understanding, bank on that, and think of situations that could have been or would have been.

The skills that would be addressed are as follows:

- **Metacognitive awareness:** What do I know? How do I approach it?
- **Self-reflection:** Do I know enough? Which principle should I read up on more?
- **Self-regulation and monitoring:** What should the keywords of my search be? Am I plagiarizing?
- **Emotional regulation:** Am I being biased? Am I relying too much on one aspect only?
- **Transfer of learning:** Which principles of physics should be addressed to support my composition?
- **Critical thinking:** How does it relate to what I have learned?
- **Knowledge integration:** How to create an abstract from a concrete experience.

Chapter 2

Vygotsky

Scaffolding

1 2 3 4

If you can arrange the jumbled pictures above in order, do I need to tell you more about scaffolding?

Complex concepts (e.g., learning how to cycle) are broken down into manageable chunks.

An activity that shows a gradual scaffold: Exploring X-rays, ribs, joints, backbone, and animal movements.

This is an activity that is sequential and scaffolded. It is designed to help students investigate the human skeletal system using X-rays, movement, and touch. They will understand how joints work, look at the features, and compare them with their understanding of the skeletal features and movement associated with the skeleton of other animals.

Class discussion: Introducing the skeletal system

The main functions of the skeletal system – protection, support, and movement – are discussed briefly.

Identifying bones via X-rays

With a focus on ribs, limbs, and backbone, show students the X-ray of a human body.

Now, the students are given an activity to identify major bones in the X-ray (e.g., femur, humerus, ribs).

Discuss why bones appear white and how important the discovery of the X-ray was.

Joint movements

Give students a diagram or model of the human skeleton. Ask students to indicate where the major joints are (e.g., hip, knee, elbow).

Students form partner groups. One group can move a joint physically, while the other group points to the joints on the diagram or the model and names the bones/joints that are being used. This could be knee bending, hinge joint, or shoulder movement, ball and socket joint.

Can you feel your own ribs?

Ask students to feel their ribs on the sides of their body. Ask them to breathe in and breathe out. The students are asked to analyze the shape and arrangement of the ribs. They are also asked to understand how the ribs move.

Additionally, you may ask the sports teacher to teach them freehand exercises that involve joint movements. The sports teacher can use the vocabulary of biology while practicing the exercises.

Students compare movement in other animals

The teacher shows skeletal images of various animals. Students are asked to identify which animals have backbones and which ones don't.

Animals with backbones	Animals without backbones

The teacher can introduce the meaning of endo- and exoskeletal after this activity.

For homework: Students can be given pictures/videos of different animals and can be told to reflect on how they move and fill up a table.

Animal name	Method of locomotion	Body parts used

When they come back to class, they are asked to share their findings as a peer discussion.

As an extension/formative assessment

Students can make a chart that compares the skeletal system and the types of movement in four different animals.

How are we working with Scaffold?

Concepts start from the basics: Explanation of a skeleton/ showing an X-ray. (The teacher explains mostly.)

Hands-on activity: Feeling of bones. (Teacher instructs students what is to be done.)

Comparison to address higher-order thinking: Teacher gives a table to fill. Students analyze and fill the table.

Creating: Culminate in an activity that ensures thorough understanding. (This is entirely done by students.)

Reciprocal Teaching

Dumb Charades

A new game in town back in my childhood. There is that one friend who knew it all. She taught us that it had to be a movie name. No one could talk. The team members could only use gestures.

She showed us how to say that the movie name had many parts, whether they were in English or Hindi, and how to gesture without moving the lips. No pointing at words written anywhere, articles, prepositions!

My head was spinning at the end of her tirade of instructions.

So we took turns to get good at it, while the others sharpened their guessing skills.

We jumbled up everything. She was fuming and telling us how clueless we were about instructions. She wrote up an instruction sheet.

We started again, each of us repeating, guessing, faltering. Then, as a collective, we learned the tricks.

Reciprocal learning is just this. Implement structured group discussions where students and teachers take turns leading, focusing on summarizing, questioning, clarifying, and predicting. This develops comprehension and critical thinking, especially in reading scientific texts.

Reciprocal Teaching in Science

In the CBSE curriculum, the world of the living with a focus on why conservation is important has been addressed. Teachers can talk about endangered species and why helping out with endangered species and their preservation are important.

There are many videos and articles available online, or otherwise, that the teacher can let the students watch/read.

Something that can be used for reciprocal teaching has been discussed below:

Message on 50 Years of Project Tiger

Project Tiger marks its 50th year, a proud milestone in conserving one of India's most iconic wildlife species. From 9 reserves at its launch to 53 today, India now holds 70% of the global tiger population, making it a global leader in tiger conservation.

Between 2010 and 2018, India doubled its tiger numbers – four years ahead of the international target. This success owes much to local and tribal communities, whose role is invaluable. Key initiatives include creating new reserves, eco-development, scientific management, mapping corridors, and wildlife healthcare. Technologies like drones, E-Eye surveillance, M-STrIPES, and camera traps have given conservation efforts fresh momentum.

Congratulations to all involved in this remarkable journey. May this anniversary inspire renewed dedication to protecting our forests, wildlife, and natural heritage.

The students are told about what is expected out of them:

- They are to summarize the main parts of the text.
- Ask each other about the content to check the other's understanding.
- Discuss misunderstandings and address confusions.
- Predict what will happen next.

The teacher first shows how it is to be done:

- They read the passage/text aloud.
- Ask questions. Help summarize it, clarify misconceptions, and predict.
- Throughout the process, the teacher explains their thought process.

Students are divided into groups of four. Each group is assigned one of the four strategies for round one.

After that, the roles are repeated.

Each student gets a chance to be a teacher, but initially, the group reads the text silently for self-understanding. When all of them have had their share of strategies addressed, the group selects who would share their findings with the class.

The summarizer: will share the summary of the group.

The questioner: will question the vague/unclarified part of the passage.

The clarifier: will clarify the confusing words, phrases, or concepts.

The predictor: will predict what could happen next.

The teacher is supposed to go around the classroom and see what guidance they need, offer help by showing how the strategy is to be conducted, and also ensure that everyone is participating.

The whole class can use Post-Its to share how this strategy helped them understand the text better.

The teacher can help:

Encourage students to remember their responsibilities, respectful group discussions. The teacher should start from easy texts and then progress to difficult texts.

Collaborative Problem-Solving

Constructing knowledge together with peer interaction is what makes collaborative problem-solving unique. Group projects where each member contributes to the task at hand is a central feature in this approach.

The topic of metals and nonmetals can be addressed. The learning objective would be to identify metals and nonmetals and associate it with objects. Active learning and activities using brainstorming can also be used in this method.

Activity: Bring different kinds of metals and nonmetals from home and state their usage.

For students just starting to learn about the topic, it is essential that they relate objects of daily use with the topic. This gives them a tangible understanding of why they need to study the topics given to them and the uses and applications of the same.

Students are asked to bring one item from home that they like and one item that they dislike. They will be asked to identify if it is a metal or a nonmetal. If it is a metal, then which one is it?

Students can perform a quick show-and-tell in the classroom. They are given a time limit as per the strength of the class.

They could also make an exhibition that has the materials laid out on the table, labeled and written what it is made of and how it is used in daily life. Students will appreciate the contribution of science in our daily life.

To aid the student's articulation, the teacher can provide a list of questions they could focus on. This is scaffolding where the student prepares the speech of show-and-tell and does not use it while speaking.

Instructions

For the class (day/date), you have to bring a small object from home that you like and another small object that you dislike.

Fill this up:

• Which object/s have you chosen? • Are they made of metal or nonmetal? • Can you identify which metal/nonmetal are these? • Name them. • What do you use this object for?
Write your answers here: -- -- -- -- -- -- -- --

Learning Communities

Have you seen your mothers or aunts or grandmothers knit? Some of them are adept at crochet as well. Where did they learn it from? Schools maybe, but often, there are mentors in their neighboring community – an aunty or a friend who taught them.

During one of my summer vacations, I saw the entire neighborhood steeped into learning crochet from someone with the expertise.

Collaboration and social learning took place in these communities, where they shared tips for a design or solved a problem in groups. The members of the group are encouraged, motivated, and inspired. The members helping the others feel empowered.

There is a sense of belonging; people are not afraid to make mistakes and feel confident when a task or a pattern comes to life. They discuss new learning techniques, stitch patterns, and creative approaches through shared projects. The feeling of togetherness and society reduces stress and builds mental well-being. There is a lot of social interaction in these communities as well.

In a classroom setting as well, we can create a sense of community by grouping tables, creating clustered desks, and promoting a sense of shared responsibility for learning.

Activity: Nametags

NAME –

MOLECULE GROUP – PHOSPHORUS 4

For the topic of atomicity, teachers can turn this into an activity that deals with being in a learning community. This activity will help students learn and retain the atomicity of selected elements.

The pedagogy largely used will be creative and cooperative learning in a classroom setting.

The nametags are defined by the number of atoms present in the molecule of the element.

Students can be given the liberty to choose partners and create a group that represents the formation of the molecule of an element. For example, a group of two students may represent oxygen.

Each group can be assigned names, like phosphorus-4.

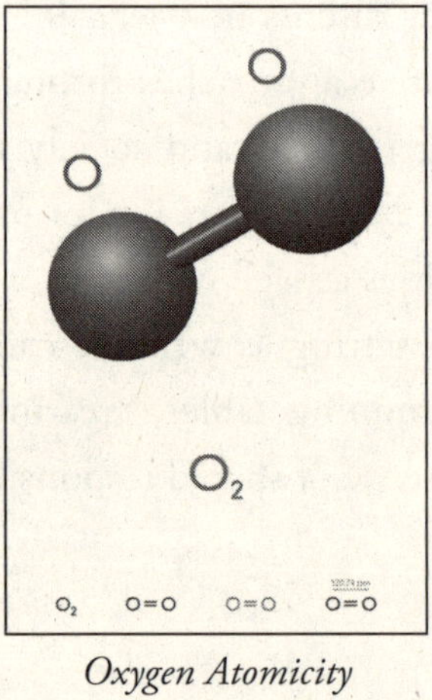

Oxygen Atomicity

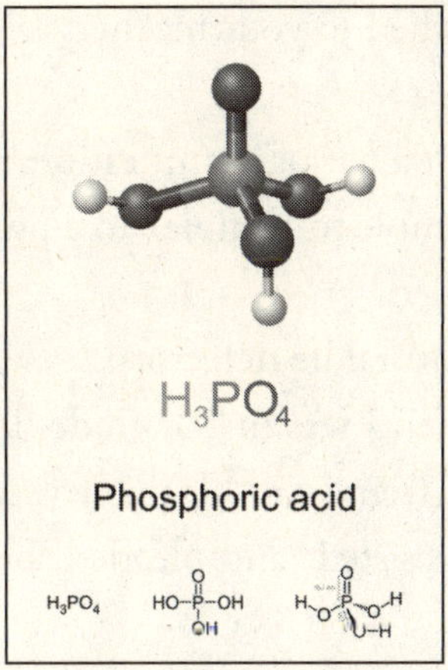

Phosphorus Atomicity

The instruction that the teacher gives would be: For the entire week, they are to sit together and go to the canteen or other classes together (wherever possible). They are to help each other with their studies and be each other's strengths.

A nametag can be made using simple paper and safety pins. Ask them to wear the tags and be in their molecule group for a week.

For the rest of the week, each group finds out different things about the element. For example, where it is found, where it is used, what its properties are, etc.

At the end of the weeklong activity, each group presents their findings and shares anecdotes about how the week went.

The format of sharing can be as creative as possible.

NEP skills addressed: Creative learning through design thinking.

Have you ever lied to your mother?

I did.

Have you faced a barrage of questions after that?

It goes from simple to complex to a point of no return if you have indeed lied.

Mothers are natural lie detectors!

So this was when I was in 7th grade. It was the norm to go and play with friends at 11 am. I was instructed to be back by 1 pm. I resisted and pleaded, but the curfew was always 1 pm!

In my endeavor to revolt, I tried to stretch the time a bit. I came back at 1:30 pm instead. Back then, we could go incognito easily – no phones. The sequence of the interrogation:

Question 1: Where were you?
Question 2: Why were you late?
Question 3: Could you not inform me?
Question 4: Why do you think it is not important to inform me?
Question 5: What should you do next time?
Question 6: What do you think will be the consequence of this?

She concluded: I know what you said is not true.

Tiered questioning is the name of the game.

In the interrogation, there were varying levels of questions:

Recall
Comprehension
Application
Analysis
Synthesis
Evaluation

Though not academically, these questions helped me go through all kinds of questions and be a better judge of what to do next. No, I did not lie about staying back again. That just does not work.

There is a topic in the CBSE curriculum: Physical and chemical changes. It helps students understand that physical and chemical changes happen all around us.

In this activity, the teacher can adopt research and observation in a group work format, and ability grouping can be used.

Students are given the following topics to research, and groups are formed:

- Activities in the rock cycle
- Activities at school
- Activities in the body/digestive system
- Activities in baking/kitchen

Students are asked to choose the group they want to work in. There should not be more than five students in a group.

A checklist is provided to the students to keep reminding them of what to look out for in their research.

How would you tell whether it's a physical or chemical change?

Look for an indication that a chemical change occurred. Signs of a chemical change include the following:

- Gas is produced. In liquids, bubbles may form.
- An odor is produced.
- The substance changes color.
- Sound is produced.
- There is a temperature change. The surroundings become either hot or cold.
- Light is produced.
- A precipitate forms.
- The change is difficult or impossible to reverse.

Format:

Questions	**Answers**
Which topic did you choose?	
Why did you choose this topic?	
Is it related to any other subject/discipline?	
Is it a physical change or a chemical change?	
Why is it a physical or chemical change?	

Questions	Answers
Was there something new that you learned?	
Have you seen this phenomenon anywhere else? Where?	
Which sources did you look up?	
How did you ensure that it is authentic?	

NEP skills addressed: Technology integration, if online research is done; multidisciplinary skills for cross-curricular integration.

Twenty-first-century skills addressed: Critical thinking, information literacy, media literacy, decision-making skills.

In this activity, the skill of analysis and inference has been addressed. The skill of critical thinking is absolutely essential when it comes to science, as scientific aptitude demands thinking in a novel way, identifying challenges, and coming to a conclusion.

What's that?

During the pandemic, the culture of OTTs rose like tsunamis. I became extremely addicted to mystery and gobbled up all kinds of crime series – Russian, American, Korean, Japanese, Indian, Middle Eastern.

It taught me so many things about secret services, different kinds of combat strategies, and, my favorite – the murder board. What is the murder board? The one who is solving the mystery pins the picture/name of the deceased. Then they pin things about his whereabouts on that day, people he met, and interactions.

And the board becomes a mesh. The strings that you see in the picture tie the relationships, coincidences, and commonalities together. As the series comes to an end, the murderer becomes more apparent on the murder board.

The topic, "effect of heat on matter", with explanation, change of state, and chemical change can be addressed here. The learning objective could be to infer how and why matter and its constituent particles behave when heated.

Creating mind maps and flowcharts has been used here.

To understand this, the kinetic theory of matter needs to be addressed. However, this theory is a network of ideas that can be linked from one to the other using a flowchart. Though kinetic theory will not be covered in classes explicitly, teachers can start building the foundation of students' understanding at this level.

The idea that substances are made of smaller particles/ molecules that vibrate – vibrations have energy – energy is related to temperature – temperature determines size/volume.

Mind maps and their uses

Students have difficulty with abstractions. Tangible and visual representations seem to help them retain concepts. A fabulous example of visually understanding interrelated concepts is a mind map or a flowchart/consequence chart.

However, it has been observed that creating mind maps flowcharts/consequence maps is challenging for students. Teachers can use the idea of **scaffolding** in order to help students learn how to create them.

In the process of scaffolding, teachers initially provide a lot of support and then, with steady mastery of the skill, the teacher reduces the support extended to the student. This works toward building confidence in students gradually.

This gradual decrease in the level of support is what constitutes the scaffolding process. Instructional scaffolding is tied to the work of psychologist Lev Vygotsky, who is well known for several important contributions to educational theory. Vygotsky coined the term "zone of proximal development".

The zone of proximal development is tied to understanding the student's prior knowledge. A teacher must identify at what level the student is so that the teacher can devise and design the process of scaffolding.

The stages of scaffolding are the same for all kinds of activities – be it simple approaches to writing answers, using scientific terms, or creating a mind map/flowchart.

Step 1: Breaking instructions into small chunks

Simple to complex

As discussed in the previous section, the zone of proximal development refers to what is known and extrapolating ideas from the vicinity of the "known" zone.

So what they know becomes the "simple" and what they are meant to learn becomes the "complex".

In this topic, students already know that substances are made up of particles or molecules. They understand that particles/molecules move according to their idea of Brownian motion. So that part is the "simple".

"Complex" would be relating the concept of kinetic energy to temperature and motion and relating the concept of energy change to change of state.

One scientific term to the next

A list of scientific terms is provided to students. Ask them to write the meaning or a relevant idea relating to each term.

For example: Intermolecular space, kinetic energy change, change of state, intermolecular force, temperature, random motion.

Step 2: Talk students through the task while they complete it

Focus on the explanation for each situation

Give them a set of questions and ask them to use the scientific terms in the explanation:

- Are the molecules moving constantly?
- What happens if the molecules start moving fast? How is a faster motion of molecules achieved in a substance?
- Which energy will help them move fast?
- How does a state change? Who does the work in the state change?
- Do you understand how energy is conserved in a state change?

Step 3: Group students to talk through the task and support each other

Thinking about the consequences or what each step relates to

Now, they relate to which concept precedes and can be linked together to provide a consequence chart.

Provide the students with a few sheets of paper and ask them to start at the left. Draw a box and write: All matter is made up of particles…

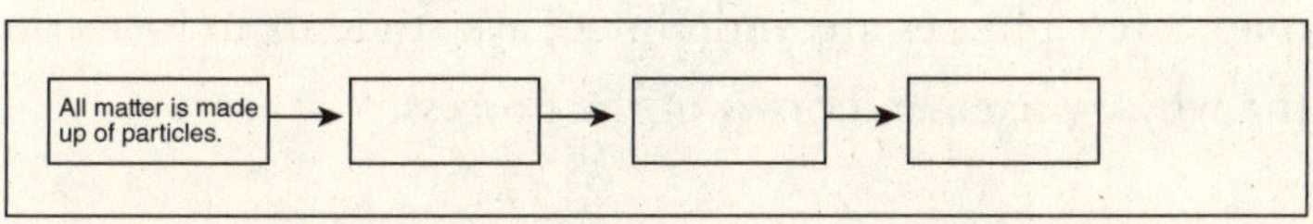

Then you may ask them **what** the particles **do** in matter.

Why do they **do** that?

What determines **how** they move?

They get an idea of asking questions and linking one with the other. This might take some time to master. The teacher must encourage and rescaffold if need be.

Referring to models of the task where students can gather additional information

Students can be given the textbook to refer to. They may be given a printout of the kinetic theory of matter from a relevant source online.

Step 4: Giving students tips and tricks while they are working through it

It goes without saying that students always have to be encouraged, given cues when they are stuck, and provided with open-ended and leading questions so that they can infer the necessary ideas from the questions posed by the teacher.

In the main process of writing down the flowchart/mind map, a few phrases are underlined; ask students to focus on the whys, whats, and hows of the process.

Chapter 3

Sociocultural Integration

School is said to represent a mini-world. Ideally, people from all cultures or most of the cultures in a region would be attending a school. This intermingling of cultures intensifies in an international school.

The concept of tolerance and accepting others' points of view has to be consciously taught to students. Teachers and their personalities come in heavily here. Students mostly learn by imitation. The way teachers conduct themselves leaves a huge impression on the students' minds.

I am sure every one of us had that idol teacher who was the ideal. You never know whose idol you are. Whatever you do, whoever you correct, criticize, or make fun of, it gives them a yardstick to measure up to.

It is imperative that we believe in a few attitudes that should not go unrectified when we do notice them.

A class rule has to be put in place and reiterated whenever students step out of the behavioral guidelines mentioned in the class rules.

A few years back, I was watching the Golden Globe Awards. Meryl Streep referred to something that was not correct. The powerful message she gave is something we, as educators, should remember, imbibe, and practice.

Sharing a part of her speech:

> Hollywood is crawling with outsiders and foreigners. If you kick 'em all out, you'll have nothing to watch but football and mixed martial arts, which are not the arts. They gave me three seconds to say this. An actor's only job is to enter the lives of people who are different from us and let you feel what that feels like. And there were many, many, many powerful performances this year that did exactly that, breathtaking, passionate work.
>
> There was one performance this year that stunned me. It sank its hooks in my heart. Not because it was good. There was nothing good about it. But it was effective and it did its job. It made its intended audience laugh and show their teeth. It was that moment when the person asking to sit in the most respected seat in our country imitated a disabled reporter, someone he outranked in privilege, power, and the capacity to fight back. It kind of broke my heart when I saw it. I still can't get it out of my head because it wasn't in a movie. It was real life.
>
> And this instinct to humiliate, when it's modeled by someone in the public platform, by someone powerful, it filters down into everybody's life, because it kind of gives permission for other people to do the same thing. Disrespect invites disrespect. Violence incites violence. When the powerful use their position to bully others, we all lose.

In the chapter on *Sources of Food*, there could be a discussion on vegetarian and nonvegetarian options.

In an Indian setting, there is sometimes a divide between children and the content of their tiffin boxes. There have been disruptions and arguments during lunchtime about who gets to sit with whom, who plays with whom, etc.

The groups should never be based on what food we eat, right?

How can we generate a discussion on this?

In a culturally rich and diverse setting like our country, discussions about food and preferences of food can lead to valuable conversations. It opens up concepts of inclusion, respect, and understanding.

The implications of food choices – whether vegetarian or non-vegetarian – should not cloud the importance of friendship and respect.

An open dialogue:

Students may be asked who their friends are.

How many people are there in their family?

What food do they enjoy?

Write the food items on the board.

Group the friends and their food preferences:

| ○Ananya | | ○Biryani |

| ○Rohan | | ○Masala Dosa |

| ○Meera | | ○Palak Paneer |

| ○Arjun | | ○Chhole Bhature |

| ○Isha | | ○Butter Chicken |

Will how they eat affect their friendships?

Open the floor for personal experiences, specifically instances where they felt discriminated against for their choice of food.

Activity: The students will be given prompts on which they have to create a storyboard.

Scenario 1:

It's evening in a small village of Assam, and Ananya Devi is stirring a pot of rice and dal over a wood fire crackling on the mud floor of her bamboo hut. She listens for the sound of her husband's voice as he makes his way back from the fields with their lean, loyal pariah dog trotting beside him.

Scenario 2:

Ravi set out before dawn on this chilly January morning with his old rifle and sickle, eager to begin the two-hour walk into the dense sal forest. He scanned the treetops for langurs and the occasional civet, while his dog sniffed the trail for signs of wild boar or spotted deer. If fortune favoured him, Ravi might come across one of the largest prizes of the jungle: a gaur, with its massive frame and curved horns, grazing quietly among the dew-laden undergrowth.

Scenario 3:

Sharmaji introduces me to a villager named Raghunath Singh, 78, who, along with his son Mohan Singh, 39, has nurtured a flourishing garden by the river for the past 30 years. Raghunath takes us along a narrow path past trees heavy with golden guavas and mangoes, clusters of bananas, and round oranges that hang like ornaments. Bright red hibiscus and wild turmeric bloom freely among rows of sugarcane and maize. "No one in the village has more fruit than Raghunath's family," says Sharmaji.

Teachers are to discuss the following:

Until agriculture took root around 10,000 years ago, people everywhere survived by hunting, gathering, and fishing. With the rise of farming, nomadic hunter-gatherers were gradually pushed away from fertile land and confined to less accessible regions. In India, they came to inhabit the dense forests of central and northeastern states, the dry stretches of Rajasthan, and the hills of the Western Ghats and the Andaman Islands. Today, only a few scattered tribal communities continue to live as hunter-gatherers.

> Amanda Henry, a paleobiologist at the Max Planck Institute for Evolutionary Anthropology in Leipzig, believes the common narrative that hunting defined humans and that meat made us human misses half the story. While meat was sought after, she explains, humans actually relied heavily on plant foods. Her research on starch granules from plants found on fossil teeth and stone tools suggests that humans may have been eating grains and tubers for at least 100,000 years—long enough to evolve the ability to digest them.

Additionally, the school can arrange for nutritional talks. The school or the teacher can invite a nutritionist who talks about different diets and healthy choices, along with their benefits. This fosters respect for both vegetarian and non-vegetarian food.

Every culture has unique practices and customs related to food, helping children appreciate their own backgrounds and those of their friends. The discussion about how it is acceptable for different people to have different choices and preferences should take place in the classroom. The choices should not define friendships or someone's worth as an individual.

Hands-On Application Tasks

In the previous school where I worked, there were tremendously creative teachers who were socially and environmentally aware. Though we spoke about conservation and reducing wastage, we were not able to address the fact that newspapers came for students but were not taken. Students read the papers and left them at school.

Day by day, the pile of newspapers kept increasing. Teachers were keeping them stacked neatly, but what do we do with them? Since environment and conservation were at the heart of the school, some teachers started brainstorming about what to do.

A marvelous plan started to grow. Teachers engaged students to make envelopes to carry their term examination answer scripts home.

The didis, as we called our helping staff, trained the students on how to make envelopes using newspapers. The students enjoyed it and also appreciated the fact that everyone got to learn something from one another.

The focus of driving a school where ideas of saving the environment are nurtured was very easily conducted through this simple activity.

In the next activity, students work with theoretical concepts and design experiences that lead to real-world applications. It is a fun project that will engage everyone.

In chemistry, the topic of the periodic table can be made fun by curating an activity of making beads and bracelets. This will reinforce active learning and the hands-on approach to learning.

Make mini bracelets of beads that have the initials of their friends.

Students can make/buy beads and write all the symbols of the periodic table (one symbol per bead). Students may also create beads from plasticine and playdough.

The entire class has to be divided into groups that can write the symbols with a permanent marker. As they write multiple symbols on beads, a repeat exercise of writing consolidates the memory of the students.

These initials will be associated with the elements that have the letters of the initials of various probable names.

For example, Anita: They choose A(m), Ni, Ta from the list of elements presented in alphabetical order. This creates a connection between the names of the elements and the symbols of the periodic table for students who are making the bracelets.

Am, americium; Ni, nickel, Ta, tantalum

Students can be asked to utilize this idea to create a greater reach to the school community and beyond. A small fundraising activity can be organized too, and the funds can be donated to an NGO.

Bead bracelets for sale!

Give students an idea of what the key aspects of planning and executing this sale are. Students should start forming a marketing plan – who should they tell about buying these beads, when should they propagate it, how should they let students know, should social media marketing be used, who would create pamphlets, and what should the USP of this sale be?

They can focus on the day, time, and place where they will be conducting this sale. A small stall to sell these articles can be provided by the school. Students make these bracelets at the live counter and explain the names of the elements and how many electrons are in the valence shell (only to the seniors). They can calculate the cost of the materials they have procured and make a little profit from the sale.

The funds collected from the profit can be utilized for service to the community.

Another pedagogical practice used here is experiential learning.

NEP skills addressed: Learning by doing, financial literacy, and entrepreneurial experience

Twenty-first-century skills addressed: Communication, collaboration, creativity, and social skills

Critical Evaluation Debates

A case of laddoos

Eight-year-old Meera stood at a kitchen table. She was determined to win the debate about eating two laddoos. Logical thinking always won at home, she had noticed.

She unknowingly used critical evaluation debates – she presented her case.

She had finished her homework, completed her assigned chores, and even cut down on her screen time. Logically, she was on the spot. The joy and comfort after a long day were really important to her. She had been a good girl. But what about health? Her family intervened. Two laddoos were more than the recommended intake for her age, and there was also fear of cavities.

It was only fair as her brother was denied sweets for not touching vegetables last week, and she too did not finish her spinach. Meera thought about a rebuttal – at least she had tried her spinach, unlike her brother. She also volunteered to fold the laundry as an add-on.

This could be a positive behavior reinforcement. So her family members agreed to one laddoo only as health comes first. However, the same rule would apply to her brother if she did not finish her vegetables next week.

Meera felt like a winner; she had learned how to negotiate with reason, empathy, and ethics.

Through such debates, it is easy to address controversial science topics; they evaluate evidence and defend their perspective.

In the chapter *Food*, this aspect of teaching strategy may be used for balanced diet.

Give them pictures, like the ones below, and ask them to create a balanced diet for themselves (growing children) for seven days of the week.

The fun is that one group has to make a chart with Indian foods and the other with international foods.

They have to keep in mind that all the categories mentioned in the pictures below are present in their.

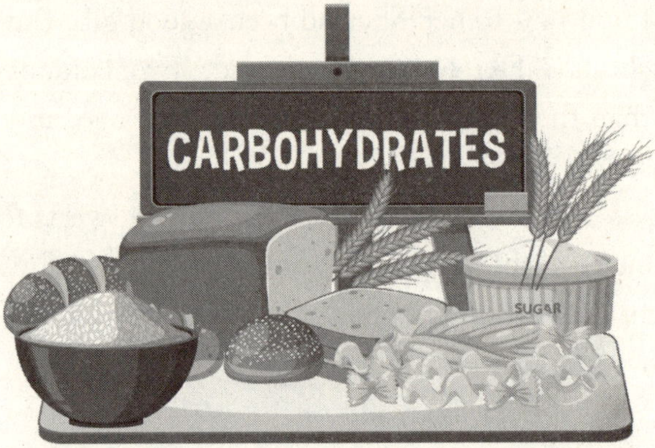
CARBOHYDRATES
SUGAR

PROTEIN

Fats

Ca
calcium

IRON

vitamin A

After this has been done, ask students to analyze and debate whose balanced diet is the best and why.

Topic: Which is the best plan?

Plan of the debate

First five minutes: The moderator introduces the plans, and each group argues whose is the best for growing children and why.

The two groups are assigned their own plan. Each group discusses nutrition, cultural relevance, ease of preparation, children's appeal, and variety.

The debate takes place for 20 minutes.

Group 1 presents their opening statements for two minutes, outlining the plan and main argument. Rebuttal can last three minutes, during which one group responds to the other. In the next two minutes, the groups summarize why their plan is the best.

The teacher then opens up the discussion for the entire class. The teacher summarizes the strengths and weaknesses of each plan, including practicality, cultural relevance, and any missing or excessive foods mentioned in the plan. They highlight why a balanced diet is important for children. Finally, there could be an activity of mixing the plans and creating something comprehensive for both plans.

Project-Based Creation

This type of approach is enjoyed by all students. They know that they can explore their creativity and engage wholeheartedly.

Here, we bring in another subject/discipline: exploring geographically. Report country-wise.

Water scarcity is a reality. Students are given a case study to understand the water crisis globally or continent-wise. Students can be given this prompt in class and asked to write a report on the crisis of water and its repercussions on human life and sustenance.

Students are asked to research any one of the following aspects: water scarcity, flooding, or water quality.

Students are given chits where these three phrases are written:

Water scarcity

Flooding

Water quality

This project goes beautifully with the concept of an interdisciplinary project – with environmental science and geography.

The science teachers and geography teachers can come up with instructional materials that help students stay on track and can divide the groups with specific roles for each.

Instructions:

- This project will look into how you have used both science and geography.
- Number of pages.
- Mode of submission (teachers can choose any one): Hard copy/soft copy/PPT/any other digital platform (Canva).
- You have been given a website that can help you start your research.
- Your group has chosen one of the topics below:
  Water scarcity
  Flooding
  Water quality
- Depending on which topic you have chosen, think about how you can assess how this affects human beings and ecology as a whole. Relate it to the geographical region you consider.
- You can also conduct comparative research between contrasting continents (climate-wise/economy-wise/development-wise).
- You may use statistics and mathematics to make your report more quantitative.
- A bibliography has to be written at the end of your project.

Teachers can give students a reflection sheet after the group project is done:

Roles that we had	
Name	**What did they do**
	Researched
	Gathered illustrations
	Wrote/prepared the report/PPT

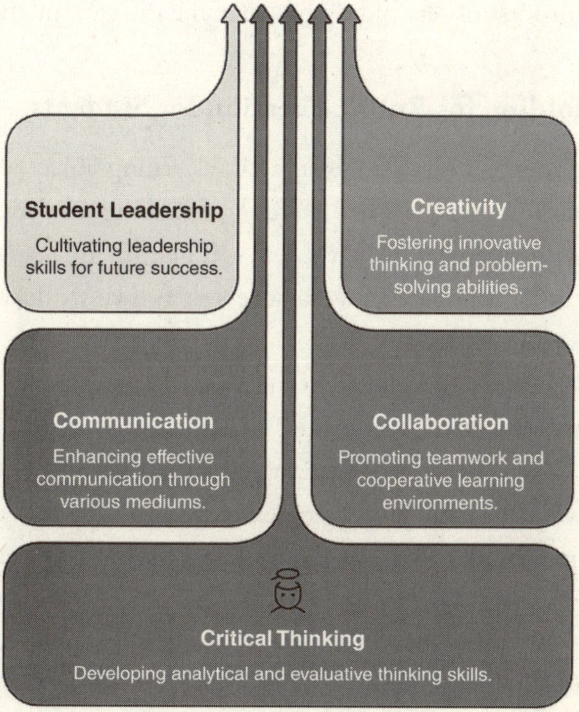

Self-Assessment Rubrics

To set their own learning goals and assess their own progress, students can align their work with Bloom's levels using rubrics.

But can you really expect children to make rubrics on their own? How would they know about the learning objectives? What about the assessment criteria? They would never be able to fully create the rubric without the help of their teachers.

A process of scaffolding has to come into the picture.

Scaffolding for Rubric Creation for Students

The students need to understand the learning objectives and the purpose of the entire exercise of making a rubric. The teacher explains that the rubrics will help them assess their own understanding. They can assess their own work and the work of their peers.

The topic would be a cell model or diagram.

The students are informed that they are being assessed on accuracy, function, creativity, and explanation. The next step would be to give them examples of how to analyze the quality of the work. Understand that many learning objectives will be addressed here.

Show them diagrams of cell models or diagrams of different qualities, pointing out the basic differences between them. They could be categorized as excellent, basic, needs improvement, or incomplete.

Turn the discussion into group discussions: Help and guide them to identify specific features (labeling/explanations/presentation):

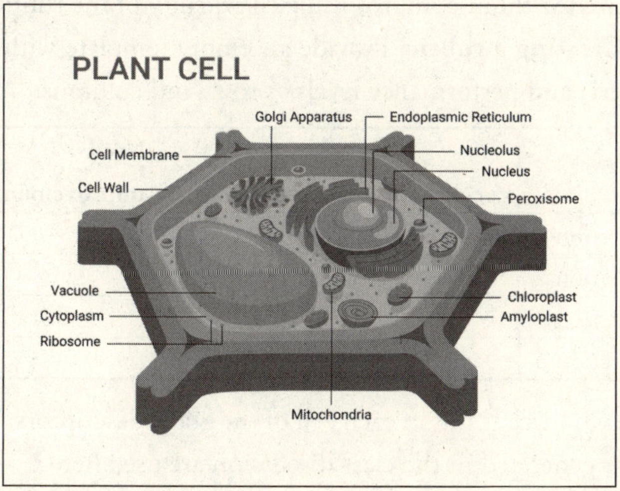

The students then engage in a whole-class **brainstorming assessment criteria** finalization activity with questions like: What are the aspects we are looking for in a good plant cell model/diagram? All student responses are written on the board.

Grouping the criteria: Help the students think of how the criteria can be grouped whether it is explanation, function, creativity, or accuracy.

Defining the performance level comes in after this, where we start with excellent, good, satisfactory, and needs improvement. Each criterion should have grade descriptors.

At each level, student-friendly language needs to be adapted without compromising the quality of the rubric.

Creating a rubric: Provide an empty template with the criteria and performance levels as rows and columns:

	Excellent	**Good**	**Satisfactory**	**Needs improvement**
Criterion 1				
Criterion 2				
Criterion 3				
Criterion 4				

The whole class fills in each cell of the grade descriptors. The ideas generated in the class discussion are used here.

The whole-class review: Ask students whether anything is missing and if everything is clear. There may need to be adjustments when students give you feedback. Be open to students' feedback and adjust the rubric as you deem fit.

A short practice: Have the students look at the examples that you provided earlier and ask them to assess them using the newly made rubric.

Students are now ready to do a peer review.

Things to consider:

- Use student-friendly language and less jargon.
- Involve students to help build agency. This improves the quality of their ownership of their work and their understanding.

- Focus on main learning goals and make the rubric simple.
- Model and provide a clear understanding of the process with examples.

Students' active involvement and engagement ensure that they understand the rubric as a tool for self-assessment.

Reflection Journals

Journaling is an endangered art. Sit down writing in a diary at the end of the day, thinking about what happened that day, and penning down the events.

The five benefits of journaling:
1. Stronger and more confident writing
2. Improved memory and problem-solving skills
3. Increased self-awareness
4. Increased motivation
5. Decreased stress

That was how diary writing was taught back in our days. Though it makes sense to have a place where you can pen down your thoughts of the day, life has changed – it has become digital. We can have a digital document or a hard copy like a notebook/diary for journaling.

I was a huge fan of journaling back in my student life. I still have some of those journals. When I revisit them, I almost laugh at myself. How innocent and naive I was! Well, it is the journey of learning.

Social media can help in journaling as well. So, when pictures from a few years ago pop up, that is revisiting what you had put up. You think about the time, the situation, and the people you were with. You almost always reflect and may be revisiting the memory and thinking about how far you have come.

This can become a conscious practice for students.

How can you bring it in? Generally, in the science curriculum, there is a spiral method in which some topics are designed. Journaling over the years on the same theme can show how understanding has progressed. The step-up over the years can nullify a lot of misconceptions.

A topic that can be addressed using this method is the periodic table.

The **learning objective** is to learn the properties of the elements of the periodic table.

Activity: Journaling the periodic table.

Since the ideas of chemistry at the beginning of class 6 are required throughout, it makes sense for students to create a one-time journal that includes all their learnings about elements and the periodic table in one place. The journal should be a hardbound one that will not wear out in a few years.

Students can maintain this journal and keep a note of all the metals they are going to learn about. There will be a guided template that they have to fill in for all metals.

Name of the metal	
Symbol	
Found in	
Valency	

According to some psychologists, writing helps with retention and memory. Students can write in their journal and also look at the way their friends are maintaining their journal. The teacher does not have to get too involved in checking for mistakes. They can very easily employ peer correction to keep track of how much the students have progressed and whether the journal is being filled out correctly.

Peer correction can also have its drawbacks. Some students may not be mindful while correcting their peers' work. Teachers have to tell them the details/answers aloud once or twice for them to be able to do their work efficiently.

NEP skills addressed: Long-term retention and deeper understanding. Discipline of maintaining a journal.

Peer Teaching

Group study was in fashion in the 90s and early 2000s. A week before every examination, friends got together at someone's place and started interrogation-like revision. One questioned the other, and the others in the group kept correcting the one answering.

Various kinds of notes, mind maps, and infographics came into the picture. Someone explained, another revised mnemonics. The friend's mother brought in tea; the students went out for a walk and then resumed studies until it was time to go.

The dynamism and confidence it gave me were unmatched.

I remember I fell ill with measles right before my bachelor's practical examination. I could not attend the group study sessions and was extremely worried. My friends came and provided me with notes, called me up, and gave me a summary of the study session.

Without peer teaching – rather, peer revising – I would not have been able to work out my practical examination well. I am incredibly grateful to my selfless friends!

Students should also understand the power of peer teaching by getting opportunities to teach. They can also reach higher-order thinking skills in this way.

The topic of why plants and animals need to breathe can be taught using peer teaching.

The teacher introduces that both plants and animals breathe, but they do so in different ways. Animals breathe in oxygen and release carbon dioxide, whereas plants take in carbon dioxide and release oxygen during the day, but also take in oxygen and release carbon dioxide at night. The ideas of photosynthesis and respiration are explained.

Ask questions like the following: Why do both plants and animals breathe? What happens when they stop?

Groupwise peer teaching: Divide them into four groups.

Group 1: Why do animals breathe? (respiration)
Group 2: Why do plants breathe? (photosynthesis and respiration)
Group 3: Compare how the breathing of plants and animals is different. (similarities/differences)
Group 4: What happens if plants and animals can't breathe?

The groups use notes and resources shared by the teacher, and textbooks to research. They present their findings to the class. This is a common feature of group work.

However, students here evaluate whether their peers have taught well. They may use the following rubric to do the same:

Category	**Question**	**Excellent (4) Always**	**Good (3) Mostly**	**Satisfactory (2) Somewhat**	**Needs Improvement (1) Not really**
Clarity/ under-standing	How clearly did your peer explain?				
	Were key concepts given importance?				
Participation/ engagement	Was your peer approachable if you had doubts?				
	Could you engage in the process, or was it just one-sided teaching?				

Category	**Question**	**Excellent (4) Always**	**Good (3) Mostly**	**Satisfactory (2) Somewhat**	**Needs Improvement (1) Not really**
How useful was it?	Did this session help you understand the concepts better?				
	Would more peer teaching be okay with you?				
Feedback (no scores)	What was the highlight of the teaching?				
	Suggest some improvements.				

Chapter 4

Maslow

Safe and Supportive Environment

When we talk about how a safe and supportive environment can help nurture a human being to reach for excellence, Malala Yousafzai comes to mind. This brave girl grew up in Pakistan, where she started advocating for girls' education. There was an assassination attempt on her as she was garnering some interest from a few quarters in her mission.

In 2012, right after she survived her assassination attempt, she found a safe space in the United Kingdom. With the support of the nurturing environment there, she was able to heal and continue with her educational pursuits; she started her activism with a greater audience on the global stage.

Malala Yousafzai

The impact she has created due to the support she received from the United Kingdom is exemplary. She has become a voice that leads girls' education worldwide. The Malala Fund was co-founded by her, ensuring 12 years of safe, free, and quality education for girls.

She is the youngest Nobel Peace Prize laureate ever.

Her story goes to show how a supportive and safe environment can empower one to make a significant positive impact on the world. Her advocacy and courage continue to inspire millions.

In classrooms, we must prioritize physical and emotional safety so that students feel secure enough to take risks academically. This quality of risk-taking comes with time, so we must ensure that the practice of firmly establishing rules and consequences exists in a classroom setting.

A way in which we could support them is by guiding them to keep their deadlines. We, as teachers, have seen many students struggle with organizing and managing their time. We can ensure that nothing of that sort happens with the activity described below.

Collaborative Report: Water from the Dawn of Civilization

Students look into another aspect of the preservation and treatment of water throughout history. Water and civilization is an idea for an interdisciplinary project between science and history.

Historically, civilization has thrived only around water bodies and rivers. Human societies continued to search for new sources of water. The cost of getting water from far-off places still poses a lot of economic strain and is extremely inconvenient for the population. Adding to this is the cost of extraction, harvesting, transportation, treatment, storage, and delivery. There is thus inevitably an economic aspect to water availability.

"This film documented and researched the technology and rehabilitation of thousand-year old underground water tunnels called qanats in countries like Syria, North Iraq, Oman, Algeria, Morocco, and Spain."

– Water from the Dawn of Civilization, Earth Sciences: UNESCO Multimedia Archives.

Teachers can help students understand the structure of a report.

Following are the parts of a report format that is most common:

1. **Executive summary:** highlights of the main report
2. **Table of Contents:** index page
3. **Introduction:** origin, essentials of the main subject
4. **Body:** main report
5. **Conclusion:** inferences, measures taken, projections
6. **References:** sources of information
7. Appendix

Steps in Report Writing: Report Writing Format Explained.

Teachers may additionally give them an "Agreement – manage your timesheet". This could help students achieve deadlines easily.

To be addressed	Completion date	Submitted to teacher	Feedback received
1. Executive summary: highlights of the main topic			
2. Table of Contents: index page			
3. Introduction: origin, essentials of the main subject			
4. Body: main report			
5. Conclusion: inferences, measures taken, projections			
6. Reference: sources of information			
7. Appendix			

Final submission date	
Signature of student	

Routine and predictability in meeting physiological needs were also addressed by Maslow.

To feel a sense of order, the students must have designated lab classes on a specific day of the week. The preparation of lab lessons must be laid down at the beginning of the year. For example, which notebook, geometry box, or the like is to be brought. This helps in curbing distraction. Post-pandemic, the amount of anxiety and restlessness among students has seen a surge. A proper routine and set of unchanging instructions will have a positive effect on students.

Parents of the students need to be spoken to with respect to the amount of sleep they get before they come to school. Students should be well-rested and have had a proper breakfast before coming to school. If these needs are unmet, proper learning will fail to happen.

Belonging Activities: Bring a Piece of Clothing

The experience of learning: Materials that animals provide – clothes and fabrics of daily use. The students are asked to explore how daily materials like clothes are connected with animals. The students will understand the concepts of practice, peer teaching, self-assessment, and belonging in groups.

The activity can be conducted in steps.

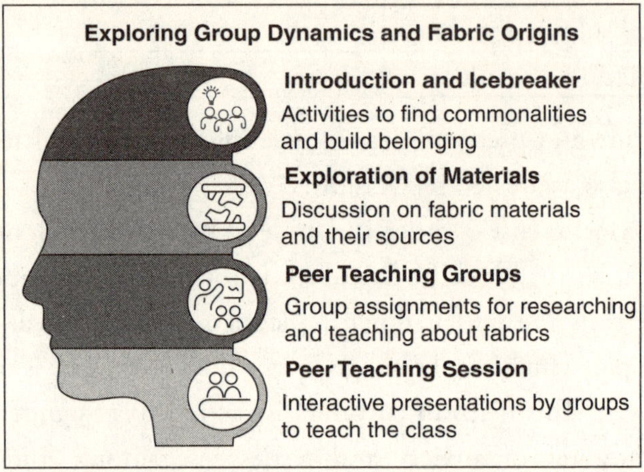

An ice-breaker would be to find commonalities. In a group activity, ask students to discuss their favorite color of clothes, type of clothes, where they are made, who buys them for them, etc. Share the common favorites and celebrate the list!

Exploration: Clothes – the materials of daily activities.

They can discuss the following questions:

What is the material your clothes are made of?

Do you know where these materials come from?

The teacher needs to come in here and help out with the names – silk, wool, cotton, nylon, leather. They can talk about how some of them come from plants and some from animals. The teacher can show samples of wool, silk, and leather. There are a lot of videos on YouTube that show the shearing of wool off sheep or how silk is produced.

The teacher may look for age-appropriate videos to explain the process of making clothing material from animals.

Peer teaching groups would come in.

Assigning groups:

Group 1: Silk from silkworms

Group 2: Wool from sheep and goats

Group 3: Leather from cows and other animals

Group 4: Other fabrics from animals (cashmere, alpaca, etc.)

Each group researches and prepares a short but creative way of teaching the class using a quiz, a poster, or a story.

In peer teaching sessions, each group presents their topic, and interactive methods like audience participation and questions from classmates are encouraged after each presentation. This works toward fostering a sense of community through students working in groups. Inclusive practices are encouraged, where every student has a role to play. This addresses students' need to belong.

Recognition and praise are regular features of any discipline. Without praising students' efforts, it is impossible to create an environment for learning. Self-esteem and motivation should be a part of science classes. Every curious question and every out-of-the-box thinking should be acknowledged and celebrated.

Choice and Autonomy

Auroville, or the City of Dawn, is an experimental township that is international in nature. It is located about 10 km north of Pondicherry and was founded by Mirra Alfassa, or "The Mother", in 1968, who was the spiritual collaborator of Aurobindo Ghosh. The designer of the township was a French architect, Roger Anger.

The unique vision of Auroville was to be a unique town where people from any country could live together in progressive harmony and peace. There would be no divisions of creed, nationality, or politics. It would be an embodiment of unity and would be known as the place for spiritual research. Human unity would be at the core of its purpose.

Auroville

In my recent visit to Auroville, what struck me the most was when my tour guide, an Aurovillian as they call themselves, told me that all of the residents work to serve the community and have to survive on a pay that seemed nominal to me. The choice that people from all over the world had made – to live in a minimalist society where indulgences of the twenty-first century were almost non-existent – was astonishing.

The population of Auroville is about 3,300 people from over 60 countries. The economy works in a unique way: the township operates without a traditional currency. Residents use Aurocards for transactions, and all earnings have a certain percentage to be given for the upkeep of the community. Schooling, healthcare, and electricity are free for residents. The education is mostly flexible and self-paced.

The Auroville Foundation consists of a governing body, an international advisory council, and a resident assembly, which includes all adult residents. Sustainable living, social innovation, and spiritual growth are at the center of this township.

The focus of the community is as follows:

- Using appropriate non-polluting technologies
- Sustainable energy systems
- Educational projects and social enterprises
- Biodiversity
- Regeneration of the environment

The unique aspect of Auroville is that it is the only internationally recognized experiment in human unity. It addresses the transformation of consciousness.

In this mostly selfish world, there are people who are spiritually invested in alternative living, sustainability, and global harmony. The idea to make this choice stems from the fact that the people are independent thinkers. They have consciously uprooted themselves from the usual ways of life and have found harmony in this alternate way of living.

To establish self-actualization, students should be allowed to make choices in their learning – be it project topics, experimental designs, etc.

One such activity is shared below:

Activity 4: Making a song/mnemonic/poem/calendar of the periodic table.

It is often difficult for students to memorize facts. There are many creative ways in which this kind of learning can be made easier. Students invest themselves in the creative exploration of writing a poem or a song. Mnemonics are also an integral part of recalling facts and can be a fun way of learning.

Another effective way of remembering the first few elements of the periodic table and the number of electrons is discussed below:

First 30 Elements of Periodic Table				
1. Hydrogen (H)	7. Nitrogen (N)	13. Aluminium (Al)	19. Potassium (K)	25. Manganese (Mg)
2. Helium (He)	8. Oxygen (O)	14. Silicon (Si)	20. Calcium (Ca)	26. Iron (Fe)
3. Lithium (Li)	9. Fluorine (F)	15. Phosphorous (P)	21. Scandium (Sc)	27. Cobalt (Co)
4. Beryllium (Be)	10. Neon (Ne)	16. Sulfur (S)	22. Titanium (Ti)	28. Nickel (Ni)
5. Boron (B)	11. Sodium (Na)	17. Chlorine (Cl)	23. Vanadium (V)	29. Copper (Cu)
6. Carbon (C)	12. Magnesium (Mg)	18. Argon (Ar)	24. Chromium (Cr)	30. Zinc (Zn)

Calendar of Elements

Each day of the month is given the corresponding name of the element. This is cleverly constructed in such a way that the number of electrons in the metal corresponds to the date of the month. For example, the 14th of the month is silicon day. Let them address each other and the teachers with *Happy Silicon Day*!

This could be done for 3-6 months for these to be consolidated in the students' mind. Students could write a line about the properties of the element. Riddles could be created about the elements and shared with the class.

10th of March – NEON DAY (As Neon has the atomic number of 10)

Mnemonics: According to the Oxford Dictionary, a mnemonic is a pattern of letters, ideas, or associations that assists in remembering something; for the first row of the table on the right, a mnemonic using the first six elements can be formed.

For example: HHLBBC: His Highness Listens (to) BBC. (The first few names of the elements in the periodic table.)

Purposeful Learning

In my career as a teacher, I have had the pleasure of leading science clubs. In one of the student discussions about the agenda of the club, the idea of tutoring came into being.

We were not talking about actual tutors but senior students of the school helping out middle school students who struggle with the subject.

We broached the topic to our principal, who was very impressed, and we set the ball rolling.

We drew up a plan for logistics, designated days, drafted emails for parents, had interviews for all senior students who would tutor, advertised on noticeboards around schools, and spoke with teachers to identify which students would be interested in taking our services (free of cost), etc.

The ones discussed above were intentional. What happened unintentionally was that the tutors started revisiting old books, and made plans, notes, and aids to teach.

The ideas that were to be implemented were so unique. Someone came up with how to learn definitions using charades, treasure hunts, formative assessments circular in nature, and much more!

The learning of the content for the tutors of my club was purposeful. They studied the content of the junior classes to identify the learning objectives. The intention was specific: to aid the junior students in achieving an understanding of topics and concepts. There were a lot of takeaways from it.

In the process of connecting science lessons to real-life applications so that students see the relevance and value of their learning, we can use the art of purposeful learning, as shown in the next activity.

The learning to be achieved was the classification of matter into solid, liquid, and gas, based on properties (shape and volume).

The pedagogy that can be used is a **flipped classroom** with experimentation.

A flipped classroom is a pedagogical model in which the student gets to know the topic at home, and it is consolidated in class. Class time is used for discussions, problem-solving, and hands-on activities.

Students are asked to observe a video from YouTube or a lecture made by the teacher or study from the book on solids, liquids, and gases.

Once they have thoroughly read this, they perform an experiment at home. The activity's objective is to let students learn the skill of observation, as mandated in natural sciences.

Students are given a comment sheet to fill in.They are asked to note what happens in the experiment that they have to conduct at home. (The teacher can also demonstrate this while students note down their observations in the comment sheet. This will not act as a flipped classroom.)

Instructions to students:

With the help of an adult, conduct the following experiment and fill in the comment sheet given to you. (Alternatively, students can copy the format of the comment sheet in their notebook and fill it in.)

1. Take a medium-sized steel utensil and fill it halfway with water. Put it in a freezer and allow it to freeze.
2. Once it freezes, take it out and fill in the comment sheet corresponding to the row stating "ice".
3. Allow the ice to melt, or you may heat it gently until it becomes water. Now fill in the comment sheet corresponding to the row stating "water".
4. Heat the water until it starts boiling. See the vapors of water escape.

When the student comes to class, having read/watched the material and done the experiment, they are given a comment sheet to fill in.

They are asked to note what happens in the experiment they had to conduct at home.

Comment Sheet: The comment sheet below shows the different levels of questioning that can be used as differentiation. It starts off with simple recall questions and then builds up into critical thinking and analysis of their observation. Inferring from their observation/reading also caters to creative thinking.

Comment on	**Ice**	**Water**	**Vapor**
Shape (definite, free-flowing, none)			
Size (fixed, none)			
Volume (definite, fixed, none)			
Particles that make this (tightly packed, loosely packed, free-flowing)	-	-	-
Which tells us about the spaces in between molecules	-	-	-

Comment on	Ice	Water	Vapor
Also, the forces between molecules	-	-	-
What do you think happens to the structure of the matter when heated?			
What are the energy changes that are happening inside them when heated?			

When students finish the assignment, they can discuss their answers in class and make necessary connections. The teachers can guide them and help students identify the answers.

Peer assessment may be used in this case. The discussions between student groups will foster collaborative learning among students.

Digital literacy: Students can be asked to use MS Word to create tables to fill in their observations.

Their ideas about the behavior of particles in substances and heat serve as **prior knowledge testing**. Teachers can build their lesson plans based on their understanding for the next part of the curriculum.

Chapter 5

Gardner

Pluralized Instructions

Gardner recognized diverse intelligence.

A movie reference comes to mind: *Evolution*. It was a sci-fi movie. A meteor crashes deep into the desert near the town of Glen Canyon, Arizona. Wayne is a fireman trainee, and the meteor lands right on top of his car.

They take a sample, surprised by its oozing blue liquid. Ira, a college science professor, discovers that it harbors extraterrestrial single-celled nitrogen-based organisms that are multiplying exponentially. He also finds that the alien DNA has ten base pairs instead of four base pairs like in human DNA. Within a few hours, the single-celled organisms have already evolved into multi-celled organisms. This rate of evolution required millions of years on Earth.

Looking at the position of nitrogen on the periodic table, Ira figures that selenium might be poisonous to the aliens as they are nitrogen-based, just like arsenic is poisonous to Earth's lifeforms.

Ira's students, Deke and Danny, recall that selenium sulfide is the active ingredient in Head & Shoulders shampoo. An iconic line from one of the professors: "How do you know that? You don't know anything" stood out. Maybe Deke and Danny were not intelligent in the traditional sense, but they knew things that PhD holders didn't.

Common-sense thinking during distressing times is also intelligence. Recognizing diverse intelligence and not stressing on only school results and assessments is at the center of this philosophy. Intelligence is multifaceted – music, movement, social interaction. The broader range of abilities needs to be nurtured by educators as much as possible.

Differentiated instruction, flexible assessment, student-centered learning, inclusivity, and equity.

Gardner did not believe in the one-size-fits-all approach. Teaching methods and assessments need to be tailored to intelligences. Hands-on activities, art, movement, and music are needed to engage all students.

Written tests and standardized exams do not work in this approach. Projects, collaborative tasks, performances, and portfolios can better assess the strength of students.

Pluralized Education Strategies

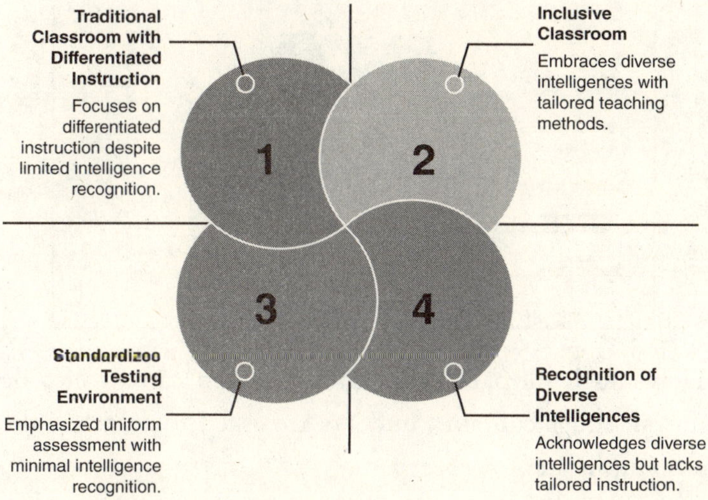

The topic of air and atmosphere with the learning objective of recalling the constituents of gases in air, applying it to mathematical applications, and integrating technology can be done using guided inquiry and integrative and constructivist approaches.

This activity is associated with the interdisciplinary intelligence of mathematics and science.

How to draw a pie chart and how much of each gas is in our lungs (lung capacity).

Students, by now, have a good understanding of how the respiratory system works.

The capacity of an adult lung is six liters.

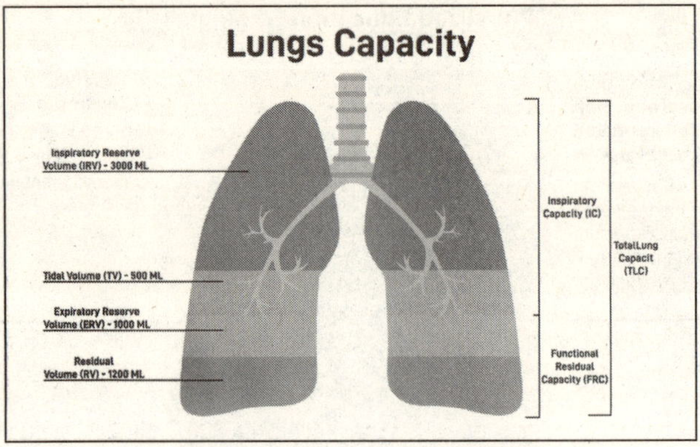

How much nitrogen, oxygen, argon, and carbon dioxide do our lungs contain? Students are asked to calculate the amount in liters:

……….. % of nitrogen = …………… liters in the lung

……….. % of oxygen = …………… liters in the lung

……….. % of carbon dioxide = …………… liters in the lung

The percentages of the constituents of air are known by all students. They also have an idea of how to draw angles.

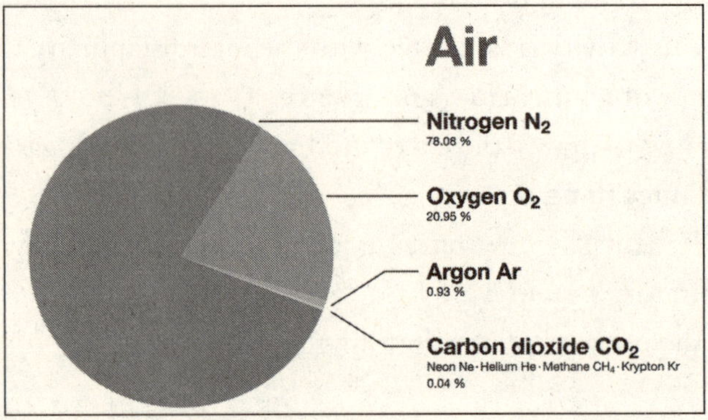

Introduction of the pie chart can be done with this activity. Teachers instruct students stepwise on how a pie chart is constructed and demonstrate how to convert percentages to degrees.

The idea of 360 degrees equal to 100% is described in detail. Each percentage is then converted to a degree and a pie chart is constructed by the students.

Students are asked to fill in this table and then draw the pie chart:

Constituent of air	**%**	**Degrees**	**Volume in liters in the lung**
Nitrogen			
Oxygen			
Carbon dioxide			
Argon			

A useful way of integrating technology is by using MS Excel and teaching students how to convert data into pie charts. This will enable them to utilize this learning in more complex or creative projects.

NEP skills addressed: Multidisciplinary cross-curricular integration of mathematics, ICT, and science. Technology integration when using MS Excel.

Twenty-first-century skills addressed: Technology literacy.

Intelligence-Based Projects

These projects tap into different intelligences. Writing stories, building models, creating a song, etc. are the general ways to use this approach.

Intelligence-based projects have been part of human evolution. When we study the Stone Age, Bronze Age, and Iron Age, we see humans using tool-making technologies that are progressively becoming more complex. The "three-age system" distinctly divided these eras by the fineness of tool-making by humans.

The Stone Age marked the idea of using stone tools, bone, and wood to enrich activities. The first mark of man starting to think of easing their work – machines.

It was a discovery that led to inventions galore. Every second of the day, we use things that started with one intelligence project in the Stone Age. Isn't that a wonder?

Stone Age Tools

Bronze Age: Another marked stage of man's intelligence came when they started complex processes of creating weapons. They understood the properties of metals, how to make metals durable, create bronze from copper and tin, etc. Imagine the curiosity that led to such remarkable achievements. No one taught them. It was a sense of inherent inquiry that helped man hunt, cut, and build using these tools.

Why have we forgotten about this aspect of mankind? The thing that has always worked. Why make little humans practice what has been learned through the ages only? When do we sharpen their curiosity?

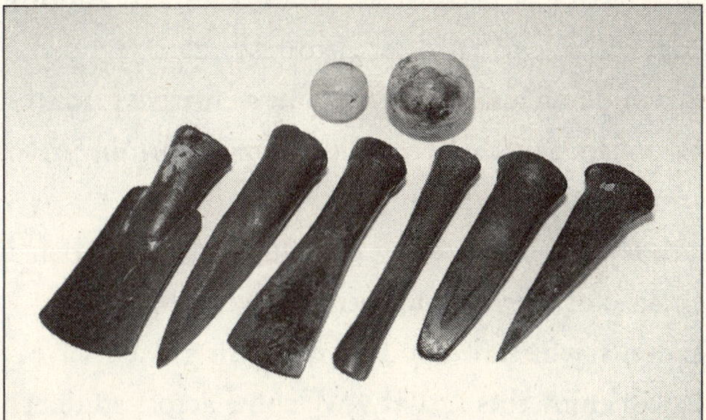

Bronze Age Tools

Iron Age: The curves, sizes, shapes, thickness – all the tools are catering to one functionality. Students would buy into the inquiry of intelligence-based projects. We need to drive it in class intentionally.

Let their brains be the tools of the inventions of tomorrow.

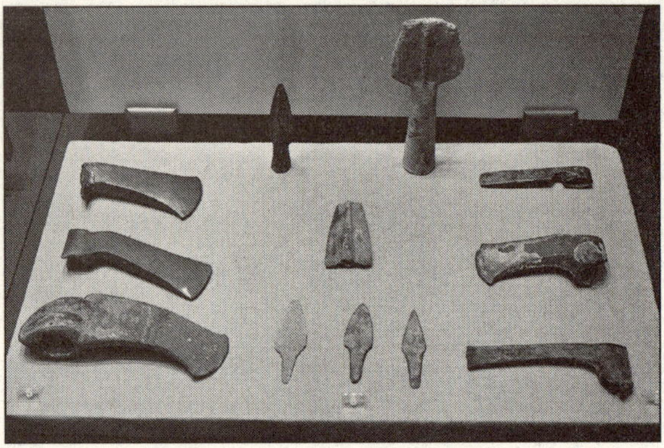

Iron Age Tools

The topic that can be addressed here is air and atmosphere.

Students are going to learn to research a few properties of gases in detail and apply them in a creative form (essay).

The pedagogy used here includes brainstorming, research, reflection, and integration.

Activity: Write an essay on what would happen if the percentages of oxygen and nitrogen were flipped.

Students who are good at expressing themselves with words will enjoy this activity. We come across students who do not enjoy reading science. Using this activity, we can help them associate their expertise with science.

This might need three to four lessons to be completed. I would recommend not revealing the topic at the get-go as students tend to get help from home sometimes. To ensure that it is their own work, we share the instructions partially:

You have to look up and use the following details in an essay. Your essay will be marked keeping the following points in mind. The topic of the essay will be provided in the next class on…

- Jot down the properties of nitrogen and oxygen.
- Where do you see the uses of oxygen and nitrogen in nature?
- Where do you see the uses of oxygen and nitrogen in industries?
- Are there any ill effects of oxygen and nitrogen?

In this activity, not only do the students research the main constituents, but they also think about the properties of nitrogen and oxygen.

When the students have researched the points above, reveal the topic for a class assignment.

For example, the topic of the essay can be: You have to write a 500-word essay on what would happen if one day the percentages of oxygen and nitrogen were swapped?

In this activity, we would need the help of the English teachers. A rubric can help provide feedback for teachers.

In a rubric, the marking criteria are aligned with the guidelines that have been given to the students. A rough draft of a rubric is given below:

Criterion	Explicitly addressed	Partially addressed	Implicitly expressed	Not addressed
Properties of nitrogen and oxygen				
Uses of oxygen and nitrogen in nature				
Uses of oxygen and nitrogen in industries				
Ill effects of oxygen and nitrogen				

Here, qualitative feedback has been used; teachers can use marks to provide quantitative feedback.

NEP skills used: Multidisciplinary cross-curricular integration. Design thinking in using creativity in one's work.

Twenty-first-century skills used: Critical thinking, communication, media literacy (while researching online), creativity.

This activity will address **cognitivism,** where students process information that they receive.

Gestalt psychology that refers to processing information as a whole can also be seen here. Students look at all the information overview and have to create a central theme for their essay where everything they have learned culminates into a whole.

This **learner-centered design** will help students connect the content and keep the context in mind.

Kolb's abstract conceptualization is used here, where the student acquires competencies and skills to apply the concepts learned.

Peer Collaboration

Group students with complementary strengths so that they can learn from each other's unique intelligences.

Activity 6: Importance of crystals in electronics, optics, pharmaceuticals, and material science.

This will be an entirely research-based project with the possibility of an industry visit.

Crystals can be used in scientific research that helps us understand the behavior of atoms and molecules in condensed matter. This, in turn, helps us understand mechanisms of crystal growth, phase transitions, and electronic properties.

Crystals are used for aesthetics in art for decorative value and also in jewelry, sculptures, and decorative objects.

Students are directed to research the industrial importance of crystals.

They are divided into five tiers:

- Electronics: Quartz and silicon are used in oscillators, ICs, and transistors.
- Optics: Polarizers, lasers, and optical fibers are used in optics.

- Pharmaceutical compounds: Purity, effectiveness, and stability.
- Material science: Semiconductors, superconductors, and alloys are used extensively in aerospace, construction, and energy.

Differentiation can be used by the ability grouping strategy.

Ability grouping is defined as the practice of grouping learners together based on their strengths and talents within a learning environment. Ability grouping experts argue that this process allows educators to customize instructional content to align better with students' needs and improve student achievement.

A little brainstorming on the part of the teachers can yield positive results. Students with different abilities are given different instructions.

Tier 1 Group: Factual

Students are asked to identify key applications in the four industries. They are asked to look up the names of companies in India that use these applications.

Tier 2 Group: Research

In this group, students are asked to research how these applications use crystals for their work.

Tier 3 Group: Planning

The students in this team plan how to tie together the findings of tier groups 1, 2, 4, and 5.

Tier 4 Group: Analysis of Findings

Here, students conduct a comparative study and explain any trends that they found in the research. They delve into similarities and differences, ethical considerations, and environmental concerns.

Tier 5 Group: Concluding and Presentation

Students in this group are good orators who devise a way to present their findings.

This strategy not only assures a very well-thought-out project, which considers in-depth understanding, but also empowers students with a sense of accomplishment as the teacher has carefully differentiated the tasks according to their ability.

This, however, poses a disadvantage. Students may complain about discrepancies in the level of engagement. Hence, it is advised that such projects are considered formative at best and be used in exhibitions or assemblies.

Chapter 6

Science Through the Arts

I cannot stress enough how science is so closely knit with the arts – be it drawing, drama, or music, we can use them to enrich learning at all times – be it physics, chemistry, or biology.

Teachers all over the world have been using songs, poems, chants, diagrams, mind maps, flowcharts, models, etc. All of these encompass what is said to be learning science through art.

Additionally, digital media/art is also being used heavily nowadays. Poster-making online and offline is an activity that students love to take up. Model-making is another such activity that is more popular in science exhibitions.

But this should not be assigned to students for the sake of enjoyment. There should be a learning objective, a tie-in to the curriculum, and a reflection that the student writes that deals with what worked and what did not.

The process skill and the product should be assessed equally.

So, as I always stress, there has to be learning both skill-wise and content-wise.

In the next activity, there is the joy of making art, but there is also the art of observation, recall, and reflection.

How could you integrate dance into your learning experience? Maybe a drama-based song that has dance choreographed into it?

The topic we are going to focus on is metals and non-metals.

The learning objective would be to create an art piece from metals and nonmetals used in daily life.

The pedagogy used is cooperative learning, integrative learning, and kinesthetic learning.

Activity: Make an artistic installation and label the parts that use metals and nonmetals.

They can come together to make a small installation for an exhibition.

As NEP2020 focuses on vocational practices, we can look at giving students exposure to art in creating an installation. They might need additional materials like adhesives or glue guns.

Through such activities, we can identify students with a creative bent of mind. Celebrating Gardner's multiple intelligence theory, we can empower young minds to think of careers that would enable them to express themselves in creative fields in the future. They could also think of how they might utilize their skills in careers that require uniqueness of construction – manufacturing and designing.

Students can stay back after school for a two-week period for one hour each day. Once the installation is finished, students label all the names of the metals and nonmetals that they have used.

A walkthrough exhibition can be curated. Here, middle school students can be allowed to take part in the walkthrough, with a form to fill out. This would work as an extension of teaching beyond the classroom.

A sample is drafted for you:

Today, we will be visiting an exhibition by…

Carefully observe the materials used. Make a note of how many metals and non-metals are used.

In the table below, write the names of three metals and two non-metals that you know most about. Write the meanings of the words luster, conduction of electricity and heat, malleability, and ductility in the second column.

Comment on the properties of each material that you have chosen. You can write whether you see these properties in the materials of the exhibition.

Give the students helping words such as luster, malleability, ductility, and the state it is in, identifying the metals (if not labeled).

Property	**Meaning/ definition**	**Material 1**	**Material 2**	**Material 3**	**Material 4**	**Material 5**
Luster						
Conduction of electricity and heat						
Malleability						
Ductility						

For homework, students can be asked to research the materials that they have noted down.

Property	Material 1	Material 2	Material 3	Material 4	Material 5
Melting point					
Boiling point					
Density					
Strength					

This will help students reflect on what they have learned. This would build toward student agency, where they try to relate what they have seen to what they learn.

1. **Nature Walks and Outdoor Labs:** Use field trips and outdoor experiments to engage naturalist intelligence.
2. **Personal Reflection Journals:** Encourage intrapersonal intelligence by having students reflect on their learning and science interests.

Debate and Discussion

Being a movie buff, I am always engaged in any cerebral movie that has something to think about, critically analyze, and solve. So, mystery thrillers are my go-to movies when I want to enjoy an engaging one. One of my top picks is *A Few Good Men*.

The last 15-30 minutes show absolute grit. The research is carefully thought out. The debates are backed by facts. The confidence in the face of authoritative bullying is breathtaking. The highs and lows of the task at hand are beautifully captured – team-building, social and professional responsibility, patriotism, and abiding by the law are beautifully portrayed in this movie.

A learning experience that can use the intelligence of interpersonal skills through structured science lessons can lead to discussions and group problem-solving.

Comparative study of hydrogen and carbon: Debate

Lesson objective:

Class 7 or 8

In a debate, the children are expected to develop the topic to be debated on. This can be given by the teacher. Students are divided into teams, which can be grouped by ability. The teacher establishes the rules of the debate.

Students will look at the physical and chemical properties of hydrogen and carbon. They will research the uses and requirements for these gases for life and livelihood. They have to research and think about logical arguments.

Facts

Name	Hydrogen	Carbon
Atomic Number	1	6
Atomic Symbol	H	C
Atomic Weight	1.00794	12.0107
Phase at STP	Gas	Solid
Color	Colorless	Black
Metallic Classification	Other Nonmetal	Other Nonmetal
Group in Periodic Table	group 1	group 14
Group Name	lithium family	carbon family
Period in Periodic Table	period 1	period 2
Block in Periodic Table	s -block	p -block
Electronic Configuration	1s1	[He] 2s2 2p2
Electronic Shell Structure (Electrons per shell)	1	2, 4

In the process of preparing for the debate, students are supposed to:

- Gather evidence and examples that support their argument.
- Anticipate arguments from the opposing team and prepare rebuttals.
- Team members plan the content and the order of the participants.

A typical sequence for the debate, with suggested timelines, is as follows:

- The first speaker on Team Hydrogen presents arguments in support of hydrogen being the better element. (three minutes)
- The first speaker on Team Carbon presents arguments as to why he/she thinks that carbon is a better element. (three minutes)
- The second speaker on Team Hydrogen presents further arguments in support of hydrogen, identifies the weaknesses of Team Carbon, and answers questions that may have been raised by them. (two minutes)
- The second speaker on Team Carbon presents further arguments in support of carbon, identifies the weaknesses of Team Hydrogen, and answers questions that may have been raised by them. (two minutes)
- Recess is given to prepare rebuttals. (five minutes) Access to the internet may or may not be given.
- Team Carbon begins with the rebuttal. (three minutes)
- First rebuttal of Team Hydrogen. (3-5 minutes)

- Each team gets a second rebuttal for closing statements with Team Hydrogen having the last opportunity to speak. (two minutes each)
- In case of interruptions, teachers may have to enforce the rules.

This is best suited as a collaborative activity of the English and science departments. There could be two separate rubrics, each for English and science.

There could be a student poll done as well when deciding the best speaker. This could be a WhatsApp poll or a pen-and-paper poll. They could also write a line about which skill made them choose the best speaker.

Student-Centered Discussion and Debate Strategies

Characteristic	Assign Roles	Structured Format	Debrief
Purpose	Ensures active participation	Provides organized discussion framework	Allows reflection on discussion
Examples	Moderator, researchers, summarizers	Formal debate, think-pair-share	Self-reflection, peer feedback, group discussion
Tools/Techniques	None	Timers, discussion formats	Evidence-based arguments
Promoting Respect	Active listening, avoiding attacks	Model respectful behavior	Address conflict constructively

Gardner's interpersonal intelligence is used here when students interact with other students during the assembly. Students also use interpersonal skills when they try to convince a family member to adopt the pledge for the betterment of the environment.

This also serves as a **learner-centered design** where content collaboration and conversation are addressed.

Learning objective: To translate the understanding of the preservation of the environment into awareness in the school community.

Classes 7 and 8

Pedagogy used: Service learning, collaboration, brainstorming, guided inquiry, and scaffolding during the preparation of the assembly; constructivist approach in the active assembly.

Activity 5: Awareness campaign on acid rain for school

Communication

Leadership skills

Students of classes 7 and 8 are taught about the harmful consequences of emissions of greenhouse gases.

Students can plan an assembly by creating a chart/ presentation on the same.

In this activity, the teacher focuses on the learning objective so that, during the entire preparation, they keep going back to what they need to learn in their syllabus. **Acid rain is caused by emissions:** This acts as a consolidation of their learning.

In the assembly, the students who are presenting the chart or PPT describe what is happening in it by showing a picture like the one shown above. They can **prompt and ask questions** from students in the audience to engage them in the assembly. A set of probable questions can be:

- What do you see in the picture?
- Which objects in the picture can emit harmful gases?
- Why are they harmful to the environment?
- When oxides of such gases react with water vapor, what kind of substance is created?
- How could these new substances affect human living conditions?

Students can extend their learning and discuss the steps they could take to stop acid rain. They may ask students to repeat after them and take a pledge to make a difference in this regard. Further, they could ask them to talk about acid rain to any one member of the family and keep the chain of awareness going. They could convince their family to take a pledge to work for the betterment of the environment.

Post this activity, the junior school can be made to participate in a slogan-writing competition on how acid rain is formed, how it is harmful, and how it can be prevented. As in any competition, the top three students are given recognition with awards. Their slogans can be printed in the school yearbook with their photographs.

NEP skills addressed: Holistic embracing of how to care for our environment so that we can have sustainable lifestyles.

Twenty-first-century skills addressed: Creativity, collaboration, communication, social skills, global awareness, environmental awareness.

Chapter 7

Kolb

Concrete Experience Activities

Early on in my career, I was part of the ISA project conducted by the British Council.

All of us science teachers put our heads together, and the topic we chose was plastic disposal and how it affects waterbodies.

In one part of the project, our students had to go to the neighborhood of the school where there was a local pond. No matter how much our government tried, there were people who threw garbage in it. The students went and had discussions with all the people who were residing in that area. They got to see the mosquitoes breeding in the stagnant water and informed the residents about it.

The energy of the students rubbed off on the residents, who said that they would take care of the pond so that they could live in a clean and hygienic space.

My students had concrete experience of applying what they had learned to make a bit of difference. Whenever I meet them, they still talk about it.

The concept that can be taught using this approach is arrangement of atoms/molecules in solids, liquids, and gases.

Intermolecular space, cohesive forces

Pedagogy used here is learning by doing, visualization, and experiential learning.

Students are asked to bring marbles or can make small balls by crumpling paper. This could be used as molecules. They may use newspaper/Papier Mache/used paper from old books and aid in recycling to foster a sense of sustainability.

Since NEP also talks about vocational courses, involving the art teacher to help students learn how to make Papier Mache can be a foundational step to get into creating crafts and can engage students into building installations and sculpting.

Step 1

Each student takes a few marbles/balls and uses adhesive to create the structure of a solid. They are given the idea that it has to be tightly packed.

Put this structure in a bowl.

Step 2

For the next part of the activity, ask students to bring a simple thread spool or wool.

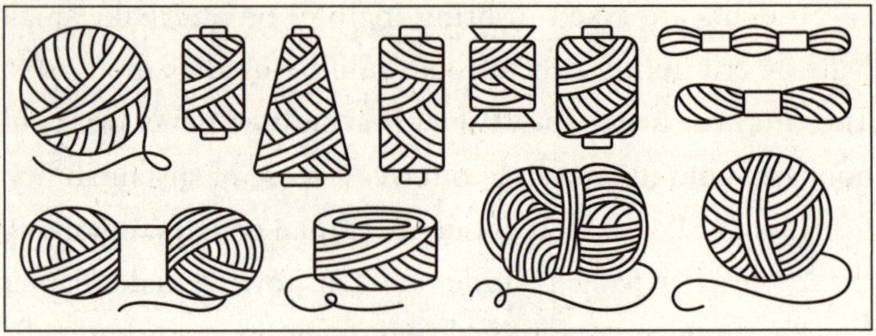

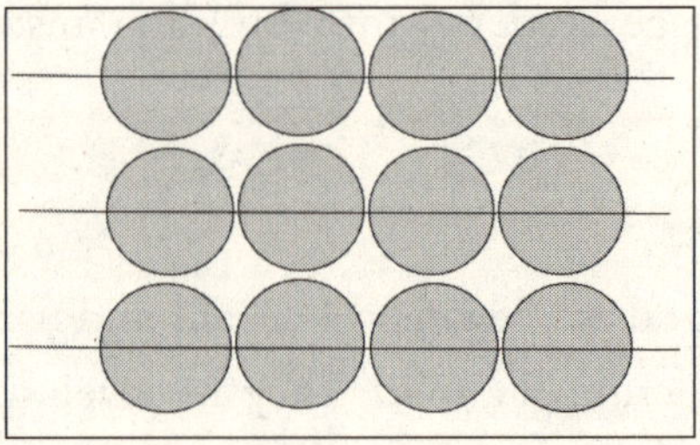

They are also asked to bring small circles cut from paper.

They stick the circular papers on the string next to each other. They make many such rows, as shown in the image. All the rows of strings or wool are to be put in a bowl.

Step 3

For the next part of the activity, the students are asked to bring a tray and keep the marbles loose on the tray.

They are asked to observe all the three structures and ponder on the questions given.

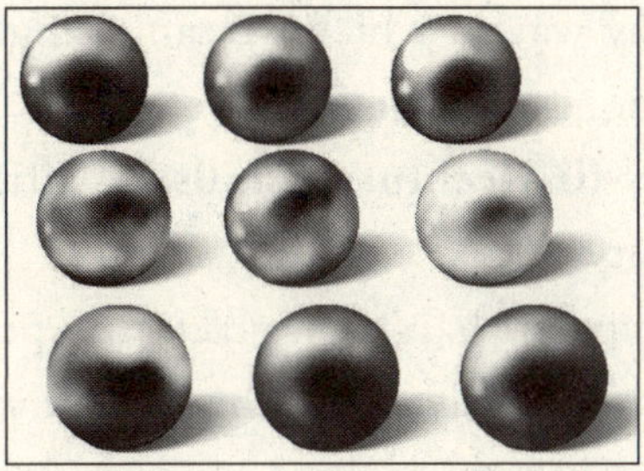

Step 4

The questions could be typed on paper/written on the board/ shown via a projector. The questions have to be visible for the entire lesson.

1. What do you think each structure represents?
2. Comment on the structure of each structure.
3. Do they flow?
4. What can you say about the distance between the marbles/circles?
5. Rank the force of attraction between the marbles and circles.
6. Do you think the forces have something to do with the way they flow?
7. What do you think happens to the forces as they change from one state of matter to the other?
8. What energy helps them change from solid to liquid to gas?
9. What energy helps them change from gas to liquid to solid?

10. Is there any way in which we can change the forces in solids without changing its state?
    - **Twenty-first-century skills:** Critical thinking, flexibility.
    - **NEP** suggests hands-on practical experimentation.
    - This is the active experimentation part of **Kolb's** experimentation, where students plan, test, and make decisions.

Both activities 1 and 2 have a well-defined focus on stimulating critical thinking. The questions the students need to answer go beyond the purpose of differentiation and also lay the groundwork for testing prior knowledge for the upcoming part of the curriculum. Differentiation in group work is essential as challenging questions will keep the students with higher-order thinking skills engaged.

Since the effect of heat and energy is introduced as critical thinking, students start thinking about how materials behave with temperature changes. The concept of kinetic energy and the vibration of particles can be subtly nudged into their understanding.

Reflective Observation

Switching off the lights and fans has always been an issue… at home and sometimes in school. No amount of interventions, consequences, or harsh reminders did the trick. So, we got into our groups and thought of an effective way.

Suggestions galore – make them write 100 times: "I am going to switch off the fans and lights"; stay back for 30 minutes, etc. We all knew in our hearts that it would work for a few days, but there would need to be reminders and some adult being in charge.

Change of perspective: Could it be something that students enjoyed?

We talk and harp on student agency so much – they should be in charge of such rectification in attitude…

So we came up with a chant:

"We look to the left.
We look to the right.
Take a bit of pause.
Does it look bright?
Is there a draft?
Are there lights?
Then you know what to do,
To make tomorrow remain bright."

Make this a habit before dispersing the class every day. This becomes the culture of the school. They do the needful with a hearty laugh!

When it comes to addressing any crisis – be it natural resources or the climate – the most important thing to remember is how we ensure that the children learn about the cost of not being informed. They, in turn, should be agents of change. The enthusiasm of young minds should be put to use in enabling them to propagate the message of concern. In this section, some strategies will be discussed that could not only be used here but also for any such content taught to students.

Comprehension and group discussion in ways water is wasted in our daily lives

Often, things that are readily available to us go unappreciated. Ask students to discuss the ways they think water is wasted in their daily lives. The teacher lists it down on the board and adds some of his/her own.

Students are told that they are going to read an article, answer some questions, and participate in a discussion.

In this activity, children are going to get a printout of the following article:

> ### A Clean Water Crisis
>
> The water you drink today has likely been around in one form or another since dinosaurs roamed the Earth, hundreds of millions of years ago.
>
> While the amount of freshwater on the planet has remained fairly constant over time —continually recycled through the atmosphere and back into our cups—the population has exploded. This means that every year competition for a clean, copious supply of water for drinking, cooking, bathing, and sustaining life intensifies.
>
> Water scarcity is an abstract concept to many and a stark reality for others. It is the result of myriad environmental, political, economic, and social forces.
>
> Freshwater makes up a very small fraction of all water on the planet. While nearly 70 percent of the world is covered by water, only 2.5 percent of it is fresh. The rest is saline and ocean-based. Even then, just 1 percent of our freshwater is easily accessible, with much of it trapped in glaciers and snowfields. In essence, only 0.007 percent of the planet's water is available to fuel and feed its 6.8 billion people.
>
> Due to geography, climate, engineering, regulation, and competition for resources,

The questions can be arranged according to Bloom's verbs:

Chapter 8

Abstract Conceptualization

The Journey to the Center of the Earth

Read this book? Jules Verne captures the imagination of both young and old. In the book, Professor Lidenbrock chances upon an ancient manuscript, and it piques his intellectual curiosity. He promises to decipher the unsolvable coded message that lies within it. His tenacity helps him decipher the story, which involves an Icelandic explorer who travels to the center of the Earth, finding his way there via a volcano.

The explorer builds a crew of men, which includes his nervous nephew, Axel. Together, they start on the adventure and face fearsome situations along the way.

In the story, the German scientist believes that there are tubes down the volcano that reach the center of the Earth. They stumble into inactive Icelandic volcanoes, where they encounter cave-ins, subpolar tornadoes, underground oceans, and prehistoric creatures from the Mesozoic and Cenozoic eras.

Eventually, they are spewed back by an active volcano in southern Italy.

This deals with the category of subterranean fiction. It is an extremely well-researched Victorian piece of science. The innovative concept of the prehistoric realm has influenced many other authors.

Guide students to connect their experiences to scientific theories, building mental models and explanations.

In the following activity, the students have creative freedom to express their interest in science with a topic in mind.

The learning objective is to research a few properties of gases in detail and apply it in a creative form (essay).

Brainstorming, research, and reflective integration should be used extensively in this activity.

Activity: Write an essay on what would happen if the percentages of oxygen and nitrogen were flipped.

Students who are good at expressing themselves using words will enjoy this activity. We come across students who do not enjoy reading science. Using this activity, we can help them associate their expertise with science.

This might need 3 to 4 lessons to be completed. I would recommend not revealing the topic at the get-go as students tend to get help from home sometimes. To ensure it is their own work, we share the instructions partially.

The instructions to be given are as follows:

You have to look up and use the following details in an essay. Your essay will be marked with the following points in mind. The topic of the essay will be provided in the next class on…

- Jot down the properties of nitrogen and oxygen.
- Where do you see the uses of oxygen and nitrogen in nature?
- Where do you see the uses of oxygen and nitrogen in industries?
- Are there any ill effects of oxygen and nitrogen?

In this activity, not only do the students research the main constituents, but also they think about the properties of nitrogen and oxygen.

When the students have researched the points above, reveal the topic for a class assignment.

For example, the topic of the essay can be:

You have to write a 500-word essay on "What would happen if one day the percentages of oxygen and nitrogen were swapped?"

In this activity, we would need the help of the English teachers. A rubric can help provide feedback for teachers.

In a rubric, the marking criteria is aligned to the guidelines that have been given to the students.

A rough draft of a rubric is given below:

Criterion	Explicitly addressed	Partially addressed	Implicitly expressed	Not addressed
Properties of nitrogen and oxygen				
Uses of oxygen and nitrogen in nature				

Criterion	Explicitly addressed	Partially addressed	Implicitly expressed	Not addressed
Uses of oxygen and nitrogen in industries				
Ill-effects of oxygen and nitrogen				

Here, qualitative feedback has been used, teachers can use marks to provide quantitative feedback.

NEP skills used: Multidisciplinary cross-curricular integration. Design thinking in using creativity in one's work.

Twenty-first-century skills used: Critical thinking, communication, media literacy (while researching online), creativity.

This activity will address **cognitivism** where students process information they receive.

Gestalt psychology that refers to processing information as a whole can also be seen to be addressed here. Students look at all the information overview and have to create a central theme of their essay where everything they learned culminates into a whole.

This **learner-centered design** will help students in connecting the content and keep the context in mind.

Kolb's abstract conceptualization is used here where the student acquires competencies and skills to apply concepts learned.

Active Experimentation

MasterChef UK – the 70-minute invention test

How do you all relax? I have heard that many use cooking as a way of relaxing. I do better.

I watch people cook! Whether it is Sanjeev Kapoor or Nigella Lawson, I am fascinated by the sights and sounds. The process by which chefs of that stature innovate, mix up ingredients, and whip up artistic-looking dishes is something I have marveled at and tried to mimic.

No, I am not a great cook!

In the last decade, MasterChef has been a very popular culinary competition that is shown as a series.

MasterChef UK, in one of its episodes, set a theme for that day's competition – the 70-minute invention test. The episode highlights active experimentation with the participants' expertise, creativity in cooking, technical cooking skills, understanding flavor combinations, and handling pressure in a competitive environment. The key challenge was maintaining dish temperature, balancing flavors, technical cooking skills, and seasoning.

Quite an easy and open challenge, right?

Imagine zeroing in on what you want to work with, having the courage to be confident and finalize a decision, and having the courage to use the skills you have, having the courage to be confident about your experimentation. Using the skills of pastry-making, spice-blending, flavor-balancing, and prep, they showed us the engagement of active experimentation.

They designed their own culinary experiences, tested them, and did not (mostly) think of failure.

Mind you – they were the most skillful chefs of the season. The judges noted the marvelous pastry filling and innovative chutney by Nisha, the undercooked fondant from David, and the subtle and elegant crab and pickled radish by Greg and praised the moisture and flavor in Erin's lemon pistachio cake but under-seasoned lamb fillet.

Active experimentation takes the form of a formative assessment in the next activity dealing with oxides and elements.

The learning objective is to assess the concept of a balanced equation using a group game.

Game-based learning, peer-supported brainstorming, and behaviorism concepts are used in this activity.

Activity: Draw different combinations of chemicals with oxygen to create oxides using charts or sticking (word equation).

This activity will act as a formative assessment.

Formative assessments are conducted to assess learning. It is to estimate whether students are understanding the concepts taught in class. It gives teachers an idea of which students need reinforcement and which students need advanced levels of learning. Teachers can curate their lesson plans for future classes to plan differentiation strategies.

One strategy that always works is peer learning. Students have a lot of social commonality; they give relevant examples and also know how to simplify explanations in a friendly demeanor.

Teachers ask students to make chits of paper. On some, they write elements such as Na, K, Mg, Al, and S and many chits with O_2 written on them.

Teachers ask students to make as many chemical reactions as possible and look at balancing the equations. The product should be oxides, and the reactants should be simple elements and oxygen.

Students work in groups and help each other and arrange the chits on their desk to show the assembled equations.

The teacher goes around the class and rectifies any mistakes made.

In such an exciting game, where children want to prove their understanding, oftentimes, the class may get disruptive. Marks can be deducted for behavior, and the most well-behaved group is announced as winners even if they came in second or third.

They copy all the rectified equations in class. At home, they write the word equations for consolidation.

NEP skills addressed: Design thinking in problem-solving.

Twenty-first-century skills addressed: Collaboration, communication, social skills, time management, and critical thinking.

This is a traditional approach where **subject-centered design** is addressed.

Rosenshine's principles. Checking students' understanding and obtaining a high success rate can be seen here.

Kolb's active experimentation. Decision-making skills are seen here.

Flexible Entry Points

Students are allowed to start at different stages of their learning. This will be based on their own strengths and weaknesses.

Lining organisms and their diversity (habitat): Plan for flexible entry points.

Students in this approach can start learning from the stage that best suits them. Their preference is of importance. This learning model is flexible and stresses on choice, autonomy, and personalized pathways. We can recall habitats and diversity of living organisms; we use Kolb's experiential learning cycle as a framework.

Designing Flexible Entry Points

Concrete experience: Plan an activity: Scavenger hunt: The world full of life.

Students stand in a circle. They represent a different organism or element (water/shelter). They pass a string and show the interconnectedness of an ecological relationship.

Reflective observation: Think, pair, share.

Students share their recent observations about the habitats of different living organisms. They may share stories or observations verbally. Some students may prefer to draw or write about their experiences.

There could be a field visit or a short video shown that could trigger their ideas for sharing their observations on how organisms adapt to their habitat.

Abstract conceptualization: Students begin reading an assignment or listening to a lecture by the teacher on organisms and their habitats. This is for students who prefer a structured format of learning. They can create a chart comparing the different habitats of living organisms.

Active experimentation: Presentations or mini presentations.

Students create their posters and apply their understanding. It could be digital presentations, stories, and videos about an organism and its habitat. Learning by doing and creating products from knowledge is considered here.

The following infographic shows how to achieve flexible entry points:

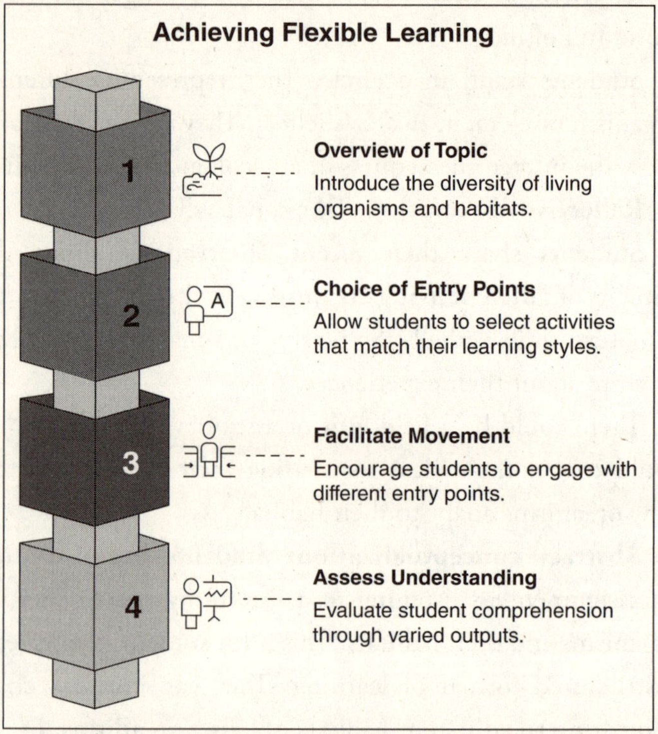

How do we support diverse learners?

Teachers have to provide resources for each entry point, encourage collaborative activities, and use formative assessments to gauge student understanding. Resources such as digital tools, hands-on materials, readings, and videos have to be made available. Peer learning and ability grouping encourage collaboration.

Regular check-ins and monitoring progress alongside providing feedback form the foundation of formative assessments.

Chapter 9

Skinner

Skinner has always spoken about behavior and how to manage student behavior: what motivates them and what helps them develop agency. How teachers can integrate the concepts laid down by Skinner has been in the school system for ages.

However, let me shed a bit of light on it.

A participation, an initiative shown, and continuous desired behavior exhibited by a student all call for rewards for **positive reinforcement.** Teachers have always used praise for such acts in students.

A new yet not much-used idea is that of **negative reinforcement** – where you reduce unpleasant tasks; excusing them from a set of repetitive homework could be one such example: maybe just the objective parts and not the long answers for one day. They could be assigned as overseers of a group discussion and report their findings from the discussion to the teacher. They may not want to actively participate in the discussion.

Shaping is very similar to scaffolding, where students are given reinforcements to master a complex science task, like building a working model or steps to conduct an experiment.

Want to sit next to your friend? Use your token.

Want to reissue a library book for three weeks? Use your token.

Want to bring in a bit of junk food thrice a week (for only a week)? Use your token.

Token economy is when a system is implemented and students earn tokens for positive behaviors. For sciences, it could be privileges like attending a seminar or a workshop for free. It is absolutely up to the school.

Whenever something happens out of the blue, something that is not in tune with the ethos of the classroom, rules and regulations have to be revisited. A class rule needs to be followed.

Continuous reinforcement and **intermittent reinforcement** seal the importance of how essential it is to follow class rules. It makes the class more settled, and hence, teachers may easily conduct lessons. Intermittent reinforcement is also on the same lines. When the behaviors are set, the reinforcement required is less frequent. This keeps the rules in the students' memory.

Class behavior expectations come in heavily when students are working in the lab. Safety of students is of utmost importance. Communication of desired behavior should be a mandatory feature in every science laboratory.

Obvious motivators like medals, certificates, and grades work as **secondary reinforcers** along with primary rewards.

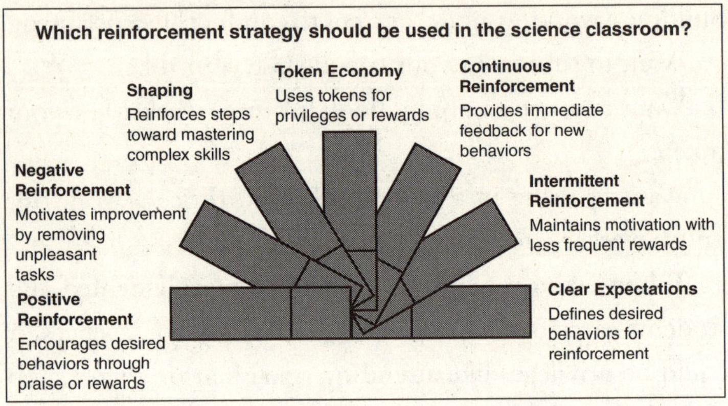

Rogers

Student-Centered Learning

A movie comes to mind. It is for teenagers ideally, but I still watch it whenever I get the time – *Ice Princess.*

It is the story of Casey Carlyle, a talented and goal-oriented science student who is pursuing a scholarship to Harvard University. She is preparing for a summer project about physics. She focuses on figure-skating and decides to look into the dynamics of figure-skating as her project. This turns out to be an activity she has always liked. She starts to try and improve her own skating and apply physics to it.

In the process, she discovers her love for skating. Her focus starts shifting from physics to making it big in the world of figure-skating, which creates a rift with her mother who wants her to focus on physics. On the other hand, the figure-skating coach wants her daughter to excel at skating, but that is not the daughter's dream.

In the end, these two teenagers choose and convince their mothers about their own interest and choices in learning.

Ben Mardell is the former project director of the *Pedagogy of Play*, a collaboration with the LEGO Foundation and the International School of Billund, exploring how play can have a central part in children's learning in school. Ben has been associated with Project Zero since 1999, initially as a researcher on the Making Learning Visible (MLV) project and has helped co-author *Making Learning Visible: Children as Individual and Group Learners and Making Teaching Visible: Documentation of Individual and Group Learning as Professional Development*.

In Ben Mardell's heartfelt tribute, he talks about Carlina Rinaldi, who passed away recently after contributing immensely to democratic education, pedagogy of listening, and children and teachers as researchers.

He writes:

I have other precious memories of Carlina. Of the time she entirely shifted how I think about democratic education during a conversation with Steve Seidel. Carlina said, "You Americans think educating for democracy is just about kids voting. It is about dialogue and exchange and learning how to be in a community."

Allowing students to choose topics and projects based on their interests helps fuel intrinsic motivation and fosters autonomy.

One such activity could be filtration, evaporation, sedimentation, decantation, sublimation, sieving, and magnetic separation in daily life – project-based processes in the kitchen.

The students already know about the processes in this activity. We focus on the analytical skills of the child and association skills in real life.

Teachers may ask all kinds of questions for a quick recap of the processes. One of them could be: identify the separation process in the mixture and write a short note on the same.

Furthermore, the teacher may give the students an observation sheet and ask them to fill in the activities where they see these processes put to use at home. The teacher can also provide a hint by saying that these processes mostly take place in the kitchen.

The things that the teacher might include are as follows:

- The place where you observe.
- Identify the process of separation.
- Describe the process in details.
- Click a picture of the process and stick it in the sheet.

Active Listening and Empathy: Model and encourage empathetic communication, ensuring that students feel heard and valued in class discussions.

How many students attend your classes? If it is more than 50 to 55, I wonder how you manage to remember the individual needs!

For some teachers, parent-teacher meetings are full of anxieties. It was the same for me the first time. I was very well prepared. Wrote down all the achievements and accomplishments of the students. The areas where the child needed support and improvements.

What I learned in the PTM:

Teachers need to sit quietly and listen. The parents and students have so many things to tell you. Mostly, the problems you are facing with the child are the same as those the parents are facing as well.

That opens up an entire path to take things forward. Parents understand that the teacher has their child's best interests in mind. Together, the team helps the child move on a learning curve, upward.

This cooperation only comes when the teacher and parents are actively listening to each other. It does not bring in the feeling of teacher versus parent. Empathy goes a long way!

Active Listening: What does it mean? It means giving the speaker undivided attention, carefully listening to what they have to say, reflecting, and then responding to what was said. This shows involvement and willingness to understand the speaker.

What shows that someone is actively listening?

Smiling and nodding, staying focused, remembering, asking questions, positive reinforcement.

If you want to improve your listening skills, some suggestions are given below that guarantee to make you an effective listener.

Tip 1: You have to face the person who is speaking.

If you don't face the person who is speaking with you, it causes distraction to the person. Eye contact is extremely essential to engage in a conversation; otherwise, it shows disinterest. Do not look at your phone or at other people or at a television. Avoiding eye contact is not a sign of being an effective listener.

Look at them but don't scare them!

Staring at them unblinkingly is like not breathing. It creates uneasiness. The right balance has to be in place. Simply do not overthink, and relax.

There is no set measurement for how much eye contact is necessary to make the person uncomfortable. The duration is something that will help you feel naturally engaged in the conversation.

The last thing that you need to know is Do Not Interrupt.

Students are very excited when they have something in mind. How many times have we witnessed a class, where there is one student who goes "ma'am… ma'am… ma'am… ma'am…" when you ask a question? And when you do ask them, they have an entirely different answer.

They did not actively engage in the class. They should be asked to never interrupt when another person is speaking. From a very early age, students are drilled to sit quietly and listen attentively as the teacher gives instruction. Listening skills take time to develop and perfect.

In the science curriculum of CBSE, students are supposed to learn about the atom. We can give them an opportunity to practice active listening. The learning objective is to learn about the history of the structure of an atom and discovery of an atom.

Interview the Scientist

Interdisciplinary: History, English, drama (scriptwriting)

NEP has promoted interdisciplinary approaches to a topic: understanding the history behind a discovery, the struggles that an innovation requires, names of the scientists involved builds in a student a virtue of patience, empathy, and grit.

Stories of the struggles and failures of scientific discoveries should be spoken about and discussed in class to evoke a feeling of inspiration and scientific attitude among students.

The teacher asks the students to form groups. There are three scientists that each group has to interview, who made significant contributions to the discovery of atoms.

Students have to pose as the scientists and face an interview session from another group member. They are asked to research the scientists thoroughly and ask five questions about their interest and methods of discovery.

Students learn the **art of research via digital technology, communication skills, and scientific aptitude.**

Step 1: Research history

The teacher may show printouts of an infographic like the one shown below. A brief idea of the evolution of the atom and its related history needs to be known by students.

Planning and Preparation (Information literacy, idea of the timeline of scientific discoveries)

Why information literacy: NEP encourages technological integration in classrooms. It also talks about vocational courses. Both these skills require the use of the internet. Searching relevant information of a concept may seem easy, but there are certain ways in which usage of keywords makes the activity more effective.

Keywords for searching

- Using OR
  "Discovery of atoms" OR "history of the atom"
- Hyphenated phrase
  Scientist-Atom
- Searching in a website
  Site: libretext.com discovery of atom
- Using an*
  the scientists* atom

Is the information relevant?

Look at the website name. Does it have a .com, .gov, .edu attached to it? Is the website updated? Is there an author quoted? Does it have citations? Are there a lot of advertisements?

Collecting information

Students should look up the name of the scientist and pick out five key facts about the scientist, including his/her relevancy with regard to discovery of the atom. They can be asked to create a folder in the computer, where they store the downloaded document and save it with a unique name.

Interpreting It, Evaluating It, Summarizing It

Interpreting and evaluating the information and its relevance require critical thinking skills. Summarizing it requires the use of crisp vocabulary and application of the understanding of scientific terms.

Step 2: Writing the Questions: Building a Script

Students need to work in a group to identify which five aspects of the scientist they will be focusing on. This brings forth dialogue and reaching a consensus. Students also have to identify which topic would ensure that the interview remains relevant and interesting. They have to build a narrative of which aspect of the scientist's life they would start with and how they would continue.

Step 3 (Interview Skill): Building Rapport (Communication)

The skill of building a rapport is an art that will help students in all spheres of their lives. How to let go of stage fright or awkwardness in a formal setting will be addressed here.

Guiding the conversation and note-taking: Sprinkling a few anecdotes into the conversation keeps the dialogue engaging. Though these are nonacademic skills, they are essential in developing important aspects of communication. In the conversation, developing information and leading questions is also a skill that can be learned during the interview process.

Art of listening and waiting for a response: The interviewer should have the patience to wait when the interviewee pauses to think of the answer. They should not lead the interviewee or interrupt them with questions. This also builds patience and the power of self-management.

Concluding the meeting: Students should learn how to wrap up an interview, summarize it, and thank the interviewee for the same. They should also work on the vote of thanks and be good at their presentation skills and diction.

NEP skills addressed: Multidisciplinary approach for long-term retention and cross-curricular integration.

Twenty-first-century skills addressed: How to authenticate online resources (digital literacy), creative thinking.

Nondirective facilitation: Act as a facilitator rather than a director, guiding students' inquiry and exploration rather than dictating content.

Math attacks!

Have you ever been frustrated with a math problem? Oh, I am sure all of us have gone through the grind. So I approached the teacher, and she said, "I had shown this kind of problem before. It is just a little bit different."

Well, what does that mean? She would not show me how to solve it?

The simple answer was "no".

Back then, we accepted it. We went back, tried looking up what was taught, tried to fit it in with the problem at hand.

Not being able to crack the code, I went back to her again. She gave me a clue: try to take this common expression and see if you can come to a conclusion and frame it as I had taught.

That is when the bulb lit up in my head!

The topic of uses of metals and nonmetals can be aligned in a way where nondirective facilitation is used. It can start a guided inquiry and exploration:

- Why are metals and nonmetals so essential to various industries?
- Do metals decide the economy of a country?
- What role do metals play in industries and technology?

An inquiry-based learning model can be adapted here.

For inquiry-based learning, there are steps that make a structure, which helps in planning and executing the process.

For questioning: The teacher shows the students the above picture. If the teacher thinks that the class is capable of forming questions, then the students are allowed to do so. If the students are not able to come up with questions, the teacher can create a set of questions. The students choose the one they feel they are most comfortable working with.

Questions can be:

- Is there a common metal that is in high demand in both industries and technology? If so, which one, and how is it used?
- Which metal is mostly used in industries, and what is it used for?
- What is the trend in the demands of metals over the past five years?
- Which industries use aluminum?

For planning and predicting: Students can be given a guided worksheet that gives pointers about planning and predicting:

Write your question here: Which industry/technology are you focusing on? Why? Which resources are you using? Write the name of the book/website: How are you going to structure your project? How many pages?

How many images will you use? Which images will you use?
Do you have a hypothesis/prediction?
Are you going to use mathematics for your project?
Will you draw graphs?
Which other subject has been used in these findings?
How will you conclude?
Any other pointers?

For Investigation: Students have to be given short deadlines and they should report on the progress of the investigation. A combination of books and the internet can be encouraged. All resources should be noted down for the bibliography.

Students should refer to their planning document throughout the process of investigation to limit their time spent.

For recording and reporting: Students could write the project in a simple structure – introduction, body, and conclusion – with pictures.

The record and the report should answer the intended question.

There should be data quoted from reliable sources that prove their hypothesis/prediction and conclusion.

For reflection: Students should summarize how they went about conducting their findings:

- What were the challenges?
- Who helped them?

- Could they meet the deadlines?
- How can they better manage time in such future assignments?

Periodic table and commodity returns

Continue with inquiry-based teaching; start a discussion on how the production of metals affect the economy.

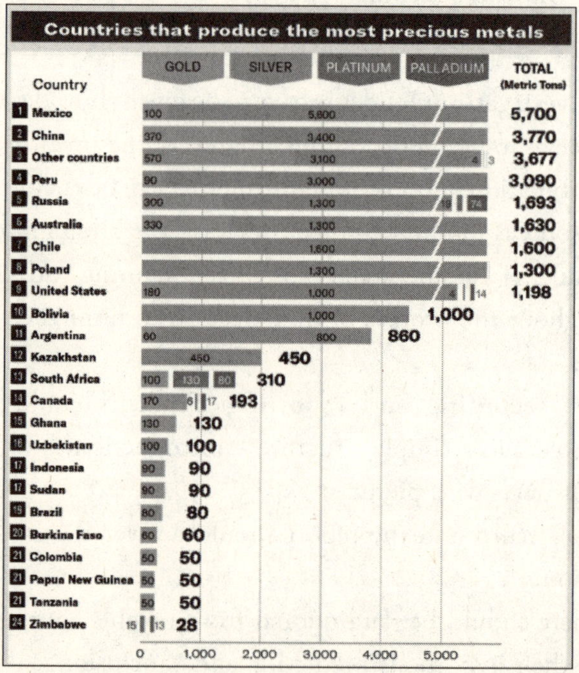

Vocabulary and terminologies related to subjects like economics and commerce are addressed here.

Zone of Proximal Development (ZPD) Activities: Identify each student's ZPD and tailor tasks that challenge them just beyond their current level, providing targeted support as needed.

This is a picture of my daughter while I am writing the book. We were vacationing in Tamil Nadu. She stood in front of me and felt the breeze blowing in from the sea. She had a hard time managing her hair and was angry at the wind. I told her to use her knowledge of geography and stand accordingly.

She made the learning personal. In our daily lives, there are so many teachable moments. When we teach the importance of water to our students, we can turn it into personalized learning through drama-based activities, where they have the autonomy to make the learning their own by coming up with scripts that are taken from their experience.

As a warm-up activity, students can be asked the following:

Why is it important to save water?

List your daily activities in which you use water.

Where do you get your water from?

What are the properties of water?

Three quarters of the Earth is water, but not all that water is usable. Ask students how much of the water on Earth is freshwater.

Tell them that if we have seven billion people on the Earth and each uses 20-30 liters of water a day, then how much are we using per day? How much are we using in a year? Let us estimate how many years we will be able to use the water available to us.

Earth is estimated to hold about 1,386,000,000 cubic kilometers of water. The breakdown of where all that water resides is estimated as follows:

- *Oceans (saline): 1,338,000,000 cubic kilometers*
- *Ice caps and glaciers (fresh): 24,064,000 cubic kilometers*
- *Groundwater (fresh and saline): 23,400,000 cubic kilometers*
- *Streams, lakes, swamps (fresh): 104,590 cubic kilometers*
- *Lakes (saline): 85,400 cubic kilometers*

- *Other – soil, atmosphere, biosphere (fresh): 330,520 cubic kilometers*

Students come up with reasons to save water. They are divided into teams and told that they have to come up with a script in order to enact a story that deals with the issue of why we need to save water.

There are a lot of things that can be addressed in this activity:

- Student leadership
- Creativity
- Communication (writing/enacting/sending an effective message across)
- Collaboration
- Critical thinking

Can you spot how we have addressed them?

Reflective Practice: Incorporate regular opportunities for students to reflect on what and how they are learning.

Oh God! I lost my keys!

Losing keys is not such a regular feature of mine. Yet, one incident stands out very clearly. It was a hot and humid May morning, and I got up at 6. My daughter, all of three years, got ready along with me. My husband had to catch an early flight and had left already.

He had very diligently let me know he was switching off his phone and was seated in the plane about to take off.

I did my chores, packed my lunch, took my bag, and opened the main door… What is happening! I was stupefied.

The iron collapsible door, just a bit beyond the main door (that you find in most Indian apartments), was locked. No, no, no! This cannot be happening! My husband had opened it and gone out to catch a flight. I did not get up at 4 am to close the gate.

Was I perhaps dreaming? Did he not go? I ran back to look at every possible place he could have been.

Nope! No trace of him!

I was getting late!

What could my next steps be…look for my keys… I went to the designated place. It was empty. My heart sank… were they in my bag? I retraced my memory linked with the key: When was the last time I had used it? Where did I keep it after using it? What could the probable locations be if I did not keep it in its usual place?

That bag, that pocket of my jeans, could it be in my locker? I had heard once that someone had kept their mobile phone in the refrigerator. Unusual, but why take chances? I opened the refrigerator … no!

I closed my eyes … breathed in … I was already late … I called my school and told them that I would be late … reason to be told later … can you imagine the excuse of not being able to find my keys?

Then the emergency services came in (read security guard and maids). They were helpful enough to get someone to break the lock! I felt so irresponsible.

No matter how much I closed my eyes, I went through the details of opening the lock last evening, step by step. I could only come the a conclusion that I had kept the keys at the designated place.

I kept on reflecting on what my usual practice was, how it could have been done better, how careless I was, and how I could improve my methods and processes.

I could attend my school in the second half.

Where did you think my keys were?

Not in a placc I had kcpt!

They were with my husband! Sleepy-eyed, he took my set of keys, thought he was leaving an empty house, locked the house and went away with my keys!

I *still live with him! :)*

Reflective practice sets into motion the consolidation of a concept recently learned. You think about it in a variety of ways.

After students have learned about supersaturation in chemistry, the teacher demonstrates how supersaturated solutions are achieved and how the process of crystallization may start. If demonstration is not possible, then the students may be shown a video:

How to Make a Supersaturated Solution

Now, the students can be arranged in groups and made to write the steps on a sheet of paper:

Students are asked: According to the kinetic theory of matter, what role does temperature play in making a supersaturated solution?

Students discuss this in their groups and come up with explanations. They can write, draw, or stick pictures to present their explanations.

The learning process is supported by connecting the kinetic theory (temperature, energy, and movement of particles).

Students get a chance to rectify misconceptions and revise their thoughts based on assessment by peers and on evidence.

There is a scope for different learning styles preferred by students to engage in the activity on their own.

In the reflection process, students can think about their own learning, which portion of the concept was misunderstood, how they interact with group dynamics and whether some self-awareness was inculcated. What could future strategies be?

Holistic Development

As teachers, we go through the personalities of so many young minds every single day. We see personalities changing into so many pleasant and bizarre forms.

A student who was acing falls back in academics as he is rejected by his peers for a small tiff. Well, it is not small and insignificant for them – it twists the plot for life for these kids.

A student who was not doing that well gets challenged, and his academics take off.

Hold on, we are not just speaking about academics; we are talking about personalities. Personalities that stay with you for life, make you go through the highs and lows of life. It determines how the student navigates their adult life, how they deal with personal and professional relationships, and how they become responsible citizens of society.

What are grades compared to these?

Money and social standing are important. How good is money if emotions can't be regulated? A high achiever not having friends, a recluse, and an average kid who can seek happiness from whatever situation is much more wholesome.

I have seen how not being socially accepted can affect the psyche of a student. The grim reality is when that becomes his identity. There is no going back from there.

Since students are at school for a lion's share of the day, it is imperative that they learn about the importance of who they are growing up to be. Their social and emotional aspects need to be addressed in the activities and interactions of the school.

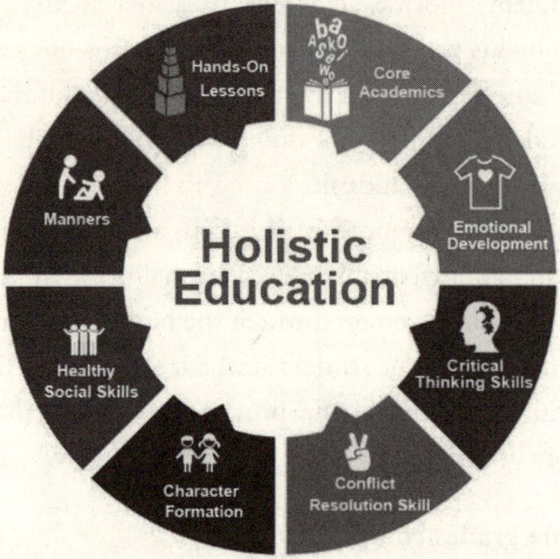

In the topic of air and atmosphere, we can use the opportunity to look into how good citizens conduct themselves. Without a rule in place, how can we make the world a better place?

The learning objective would be understanding human activities and their contribution to the carbon footprint, as well as cultural responsibility and understanding community responsibilities.

The following activity makes learning engaging and opens up the perspective of taking it out of the classroom and into society.

Activity 4: Calculating Your Carbon Footprint

The students are aware by this age that carbon dioxide emissions are the cause of both pollution and global warming.

Sustainable development goals have been the focus for the future. Students should also be aware of the SDGs.

Here, SDG 13 – climate action – will be the focus.

In this activity, students will be introduced to calculating the carbon footprint. A carbon footprint calculator helps us calculate how much greenhouse gas we emit and how it can impact the climate. There are many online carbon footprint calculators.

Taking into consideration the logistics of different schools, the mode of assignment can be varied:

- The assignment can be given as homework, where the teacher gives the instructions and the website.
- The assignment can be classwork, where a student volunteers to come in and fill in the data on the website. The website can be projected on a screen for all to see. Students will take turns determining the amount of carbon emissions that they are producing through their daily activities.
- Students can also be instructed to access this on their parents' mobile phone, make a chart, write the values in their notebook, and complete the assignment as homework.

There are many websites that help calculate the carbon footprint. An example is given below:

NEP skills addressed: Technology integration for deeper understanding, experiential learning.

Twenty-first-century skills addressed: Local and global awareness, media literacy, environmental awareness

Since I give much importance to holistic development, there is another aspect that needs to be discussed. Awareness of what is happening at a national level to develop our country can be addressed in class.

Write a report: How the government has helped bring LPG to the masses, the rules and laws regarding the use of LPG.

Pradhan Mantri Ujjwala Yojana is a scheme of the Ministry of Petroleum & Natural Gas for providing LPG connections to women from Below Poverty Line (BPL) households. The scheme was launched on 1st May 2016 in Ballia, Uttar Pradesh.

Before the Pradhan Mantri Ujjwala Yojana, predominantly urban and semiurban areas had access to LPG. The many middle class and affluent households could afford LPG. There are a lot of many health hazards associated with cooking based on fossil fuels. The WHO, in a study, stated that five lakh deaths occur in India alone due to unclean cooking fuels.

Moreover, unclean cooking fuels cause heart disease, stroke, chronic obstructive pulmonary disease, and lung cancer.

The introduction of the scheme also increased employment for rural youth in the supply chain of cooking gas.

Under the scheme, an adult woman belonging to any of the following categories is an eligible beneficiary:

- SC households
- ST households
- Pradhan Mantri Awas Yojana (Gramin)
- Most backward classes
- Antyodaya Anna Yojana (AAY)
- Tea and ex-tea garden tribes
- Forest dwellers
- People residing in islands and river islands
- SECC households (AHL TIN)
- Poor households as per the 14-point declaration
- The applicant must have attained 18 years of age
- There should not be any other LPG connections in the same household

Release of the LPG connection under this scheme shall be in the name of the woman belonging to the BPL family.

Chapter 10

ADDIE Model

Indian marriages are an elaborate project. It starts with the two parties of the bride and groom coming together and fixing a date with the elders of the family.

A grand stage of the pre-wedding preparation is when the parents or guardians of the bride or groom go to visit their relatives to invite them for the D-day.

We have had our share of relatives coming to invite us for weddings. Generally, they have a very tight schedule and try to cover about 5-10 relatives or friends' places in a day.

So this favorite cousin was getting married, and we had to have our relatives over for the formal invitation ritual. My mother and I cooked some cutlets; got snacks, ice creams, and soft drinks; and laid the table.

We were so happy about the occasion! When they came, they stayed for just five minutes. They said they had loads of food at the relative's place they had visited before us.

What a waste of so much food!

What we did not do is assess the need of the day. We treated it as any other day. We could have called them to know what their plan was, whether they were visiting others before us, and how much time they would spend with us.

Everything fits into teaching as well. You tend to repeat what they already know or give them more practice on a topic that they have already mastered. This leads to a loss of teaching time that hurts us while trying to finish the syllabus.

Clear Objectives (Design)

Planning a picnic!

The location: Beaches, parks, lakesides, mountains, or your backyard. How comfortable the place is, access to restrooms, space for group activities, and whether there are children/senior citizens in the group have to be considered.

Time: Which part of the day suits your group? The temperature and weather of the day have to be considered.

Menu: Food that is not messy can be carried to the venue easily. What kind of utensils are to be used? Food that is not easily perishable needs to be taken into consideration.

Items for fun and comfort: Sitting mats, insect repellent, sunscreen, items for small games, chairs, etc.

Plan for the post-picnic clean-up: Yes, containers for leftovers, garbage bags, and the works!

The objective has to be crisp, intentional, and value-adding. The intentional learning here would be the properties of a metal. How do you teach it? Through a skill.

Essentials of writing a CV.

CV of a Metal: What Would It Do?

Tips for creating the best curriculum vitae format

How to create an effective CV is a skill that helps students showcase their experience and expertise. It is a skill that is not taught explicitly.

The CV should be concise: One-page focus. (The student is asked to focus on only the most important properties to be shown.)

Think about the application: Each CV should be tailored to align with the requirements of the job. The skills required should be highlighted. (Here, the students should look at what makes the metal unique.)

Usage of keywords: How is the CV relevant to the job at hand? How do keywords play a role in getting you noticed?

(The scientific terminology that is being used has to be relevant and should highlight the properties of the metal with scientific intent.)

Achievements: Talk about your achievements – academic, success in projects, certifications earned. (Highlight any exceptional feature; e.g., mercury is the only liquid metal.)

In the beginning, there should be a professional summary that grabs attention. (Summarize the idea of the metal, how we use it in daily life, and its commercial uses.)

Engaging materials

Can I speak about AI?

It is not hush-hush anymore that every student who can get their hands on a mobile phone or a computer system with internet knows how to use AI.

So let us look at an AI tool that may be used to engage students.

Notebook LM generates podcasts using simple prompts. There is no human being talking; there are two voices generated that discuss the topic at length. A prompt like "generate a discussion on the impact of cutting trees in India" could work as a learning experience for a class on deforestation.

I tried one for my students where the engineering aspect of how biceps work was generated. The interactive mode of Notebook LM can be used to engage students further. The student can press the Join button, and the AI will ask what your query is or how you can come into the discussion.

Once you place the query or your point of view, it will address it, and learning will become all the more personalized. I saw students asking so many relevant questions when I used it. They could, with the help of an elder, generate this and revise it.

Though the validity of the knowledge bases may have skeptics asking questions, we can very well use it for simple topics that are not very challenging – a revision task, a reinforcement task.

When they come back to class, ask students to write in detail about their interaction with the platform – "5 questions that I asked". And see the magic unfold!

Formative Assessment

Maid mania!

In India, there is a joke, but it is wrapped around truth. Women, especially working women, can do without a husband for a few days but not without a maid.

Not intending to put down any gender biases, I have felt this truth first-hand.

When the maid calls at the time she is supposed to be working at your house, it is bad news. And when she smiles and says, "Didi, I have to go to my village for 15 days" – I can sense the collective sigh we are letting out as we read.

The worst is when you have trained her in "your ways" and she leaves without letting you know.

Then, say remarkably, you find yourself another domestic help.

How do you train her in your ways?

Back when I took charge of my household, my maid was my support system. But it was not always the case. When she was newly appointed, I told her: "Please do my dishes, sweeping, mopping, etc." We agreed to our mutual needs and demands.

The first day, I left her to do her work. When I came back, I found the dishes heaped, the bucket not in place, the vegetables cut but not put back in the refrigerator, etc.

So I told her, "Look, you did a good job, but please put the dishes back in their place after washing, the bucket should not be here, and put the vegetables in the refrigerator."

The second day... She put wet dishes back in their place, the bucket in another place, and heaped the vegetables in a tub and put it in the fridge.

Was I impressed? No!

After gritting my teeth, I thought, *Why is she like this? Doesn't she know?*

Actually, that is exactly what we do in teaching. We instruct in our own way and think that children manage to extract what we are teaching the way we want to. We fail to realize that different students learn, imbibe, and retain differently.

What can we do to bridge the gap?

If we want all students to have the same learning outcome, we must rely on formative assessment with feedback (if we want to guide them with the way they are answering) or without feedback (if we want to revisit our teaching and change a few ways of re-teaching a concept). You can use either one as per your needs.

Formative assessment is an ongoing activity that the teacher uses to gain information about students' understanding and knowledge. This information provides students with opportunities for feedback and feed-forward. This leads to progress and the identification of skills and content gaps.

The purpose:

Helps meet the needs of students.

Addresses the skills and misunderstandings not yet mastered.

Informs the teacher of the next steps.

Students get the opportunity to improve.

Learning goals can be reset.

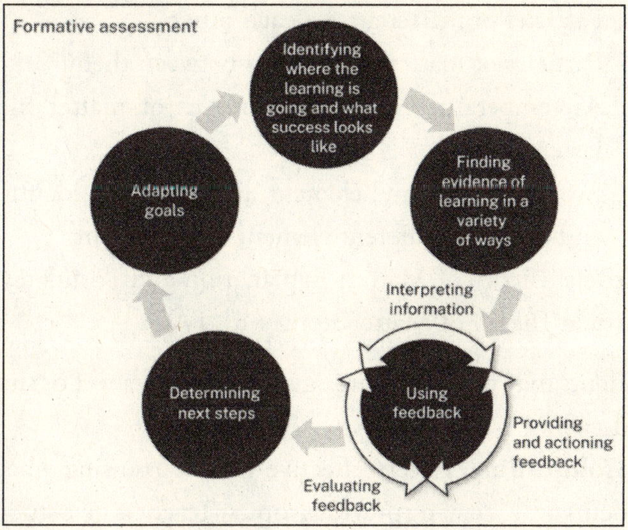

Easy ways of conducting formative assessments are quizzes, exit tickets, or quick polls to check understanding during instruction. Mostly, they are not marked as the essential idea is to revisit, reteach, and relearn.

Activity: Supersaturation: Demonstration and inference using the kinetic theory of matter to describe what is happening in the experiment.

5A: Review of what is already learned: Kinetic theory of matter

Postulates of Particle Theory of Matter

The postulates of the particle theory of matter are given as:

1. All matter is made up of tiny particles known as atoms.
2. Particles of matter are constantly in motion.
3. Particles of matter attract each other.
4. Particles of matter have spaces between them.
5. As temperature increases, particles of matter move faster.
6. Atoms of the same element are essentially identical, and atoms of different elements are different.

Particle Theory of Matter: Explanation and Postulates of Particle Theory of Matter along with FAQs

Students may be assessed using a simple worksheet or simple cold-calling.

Cold-calling: A very effective way of assessing whether students are reviewing previous topics. Teachers give students a minute to think about the question(s) and ask any student in the class. Students are discouraged from both putting up their hands and trying to answer out of turn.

Once the students have reviewed the concepts well, the teacher starts talking about solvents, solutes, and how the arrangement of particles in a solvent allows for solubility.

A quick formative assessment can be taken on this. Arrange in order:

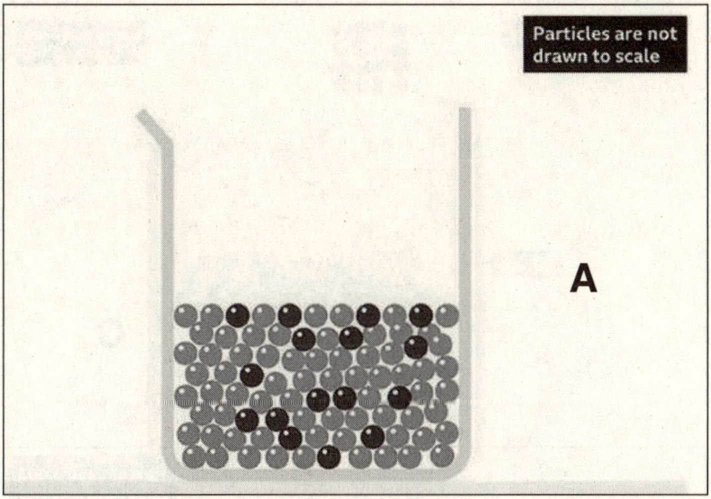
Particles are not drawn to scale
A

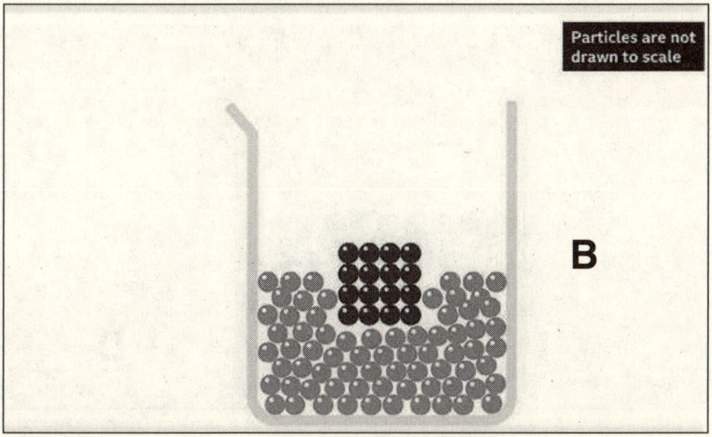
Particles are not drawn to scale
B

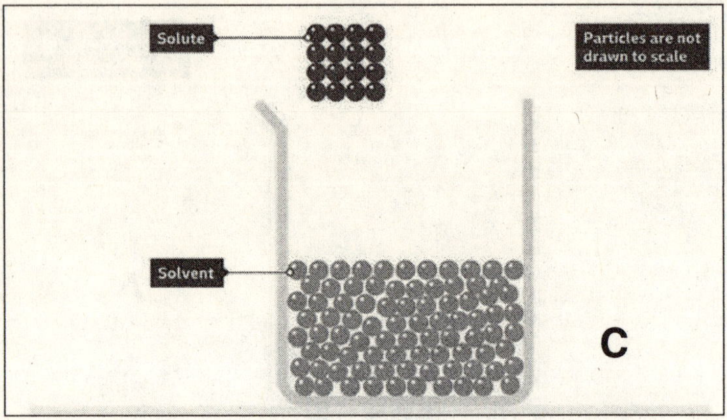

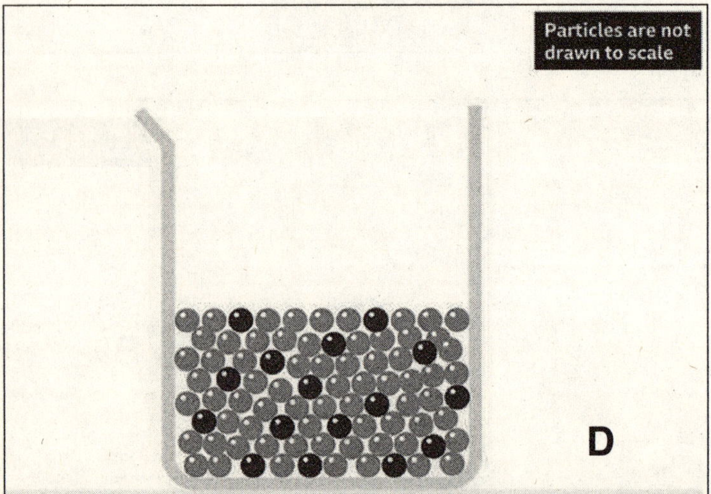

Arrange them in order				

Feedback and Revision

Her tiffin comes back unopened!

I am guilty of the same and have heard from many mothers. I felt like a failure as a new mother whose kid was going to school. What could I do for her to eat? I tried many tactics – a bit of this and that. Nothing worked. I consulted a doctor and other mothers and subscribed to a few YouTube channels.

I loved the fact that I was learning fabulous dishes. A week into my hard work, the result was the same – an unopened tiffin box.

What did I not do? Ask for feedback. Yes, even the little ones can give you feedback that will help you make a difference!

Well, what worked was sandwiches – the same ones that I was giving her but cut into four pieces. The entire portion looked overwhelming for her. The taste was never a problem!

Topic: Elements, Compounds, and Mixtures

Activity: Spot the differences (twins/pictures/atoms) and write them down after seeing the pictures of different atomic structures.

Students are shown this picture for a minute and asked (or given a worksheet to fill):

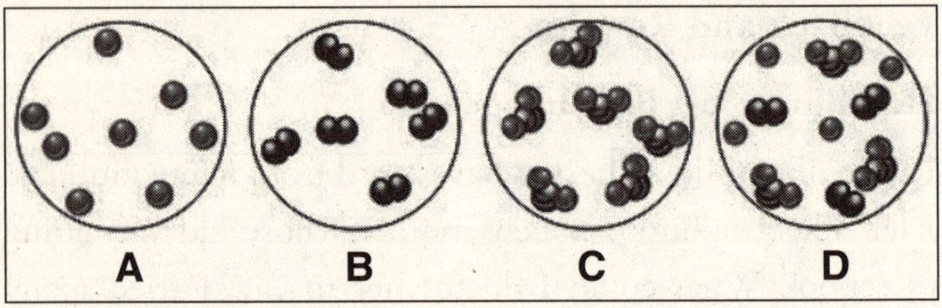

1. What is the difference between A and B?

   ____

2. What is the difference between B and C?

   ____

3. What is the difference between C and D?

   ____

The students fill in their answers and discuss them with the teacher. The teacher establishes that the small spheres are called atoms.

At this stage, the idea of atoms has already been introduced and consolidated. The teacher then defines elements, compounds, and mixtures.

Elements

An element is a pure substance that cannot be broken down into any other substance. An element is made from just one type of *atom*.

Compounds

A compound is a pure substance that is made from more than one element. In a compound, elements are chemically bonded together, which makes it very difficult to separate them.

Mixtures

A mixture is formed when two or more elements or compounds are present without being chemically bonded together.

In the pictures below, one is water and the other is carbon dioxide. Which one do you think is water and which one is carbon dioxide? Why do you say so?

Iterative Improvement

Teaching based on continuous regular collection of feedback on teaching strategies and student learning ensures iterative improvement. This includes adjusting lessons and changing activities to meet the needs of students so that there is an improvement in engagement.

We focus on plants using both vegetative and asexual reproduction. This ensures that the instruction is effective and applicable.

Initial Stages of Lesson Design

Students will:

- Know the difference between asexual and vegetative reproduction in plants.

- Learn about the significance and process of plant multiplication.
- Relate real-world applications of these methods in conservation and agriculture.

The activities may include interactive lectures, hands-on activities, group discussions, and reflection.

Introducing concepts with clear visuals and examples starts off the activity. Students are encouraged to perform the different types of vegetative propagation – bulbs, runners, or growing plants from cuttings. The different methods of asexual reproduction are compared and contrasted. Students discuss and write about these methods. They also think of ways these methods can be used in the real world.

How can feedback be collected?

There can be use of formative assessment, student feedback, peer or self-assessment for collecting feedback.

Students' understanding can be gauged using exit tickets, reflections, and short quizzes. A simpler way is to observe how students are engaged during these activities.

Students can be asked about what the strong points of the activity were, what went well, and what did not. Anonymous surveys work best here. They help gather ideas for improvement. Teachers can encourage open discussions to understand the effectiveness of the activity.

Students are encouraged to assess their peers' learning and their own. Feedback is also provided on feedback.

Students are asked to analyze and reflect. The results of the assessment are analyzed to determine whether they were successful or needed improvement. Areas where students' misunderstandings were common also need to be examined.

The teachers reflect with one another. They discuss their work together to gain additional perspectives that could improve the next time this approach is adopted. Teachers start sharing their lesson plans in their professional learning communities.

After the whole exercise of reflection on the activity, adjustments need to be made. Whether more engagement is required, more hands-on activities, activities like field trips, or speakers. If there has been a lack of understanding, more visual tools, simulations, and models may be used. If the collaboration was low, then more focused group projects need to be included.

The last stage is **testing whether the changes are effective** by observing student responses. The process of collecting feedback should be continuous after every iteration.

There are certain processes that need to have continuous check-ins – activities and lesson plans. Students have to actively participate to help improve the process as well. They need to be asked to input their ideas. Once teachers receive the feedback, their plans need to be adapted.

For this entire activity, documentation is of prime importance. Keeping the changes updated and sharing them with colleagues should be made mandatory in schools.

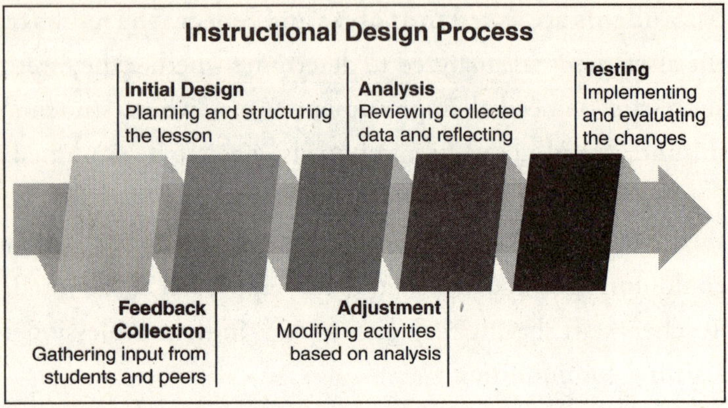

Blended Learning

This phrase has become familiar to educators in schools after the COVID-19 pandemic. That schools could run online and students could learn in that format was a pleasant surprise. In blended learning, however, we mix tech and online platforms in class instruction. Traditional classroom and digital resources make the perfect concoction for a learning experience. It breaks up the mundane and energizes the classroom ambiance. When students are given the digital resource, they are enabled to learn at their own pace. They may revisit the resource to deepen their learning and understanding.

Blended Learning Activities

Examples of certain blended learning activities could be online instruction, face-to-face interaction, digital media, collaboration and assessment. Online instruction can have interactive modules where students learn at their own level. In face-to-face learning, flower dissection with teacher guidance and interaction may be used. Video clips on pollination, fertilization, and fruit development can be shown for a visually engaging learning method. Group projects and model-making will enhance teamwork and interpersonal understanding. Digital quizzes and online portfolios track progress and provide timely feedback.

Now, let's talk about the sequence of the lessons.

The introduction would be videos that introduce pollination, fertilization, and fruit formation. There could be questions embedded in the videos that the students have to answer in order for the task to be finished. This serves as a hands-on exercise digitally.

The next step could be model-making or digital presentations. Peer feedback is essential here. It could be a Post-It wall or chart paper where everyone does a gallery walk and writes their suggestions.

In understanding the real-world implications, case studies can be used. The discussion on the importance of pollinators and of the role of fruit in the dispersal of seeds is essential.

Resources that support this approach include the following:

- Drag-and-drop activities, KWL charts, and vocabulary matching for interactive lessons.
- Digital games that reinforce learning.

Real-world videos of pollination, fertilization, and fruit development can be shown or given as a task.

Handouts and worksheets provide physical resource materials that the student can use for review and practice.

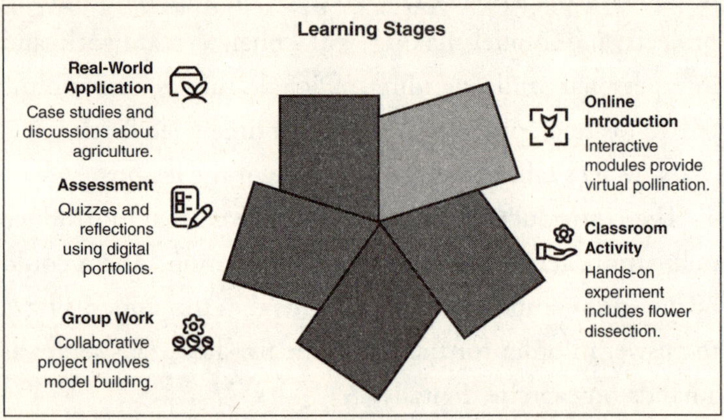

These strategies, grounded in foundational educational theories, support a rich, differentiated, and student-centered approach to middle school science.

Image Copyright Information

1. **Sherlock Holmes Shadow:** Sahan2u/Shutterstock.com
2. **Lines of Force:** Morphart Creation/Shutterstock.com
3. **Apple falling on head of Newton:** delcarmat/Shutterstock.com
4. **Iguazu Falls:** sharptoyou/Shutterstock.com
5. **Scaffolding 1:** Dviinik/Shutterstock.com
6. **Scaffolding 2:** Pavel Kobysh/Shutterstock.com
7. **Scaffolding 3:** Petr Bonek/Shutterstock.com
8. **Scaffolding 4:** MNStudio/Shutterstock.com
9. **Oxygen Atomicity:** Peter Hermes Furian/Shutterstock.com
10. **Phosphorous Atomicity:** Peter Hermes Furian/Shutterstock.com
11. **Plant Cell:** LDarin/Shutterstock.com
12. **Malala Yousafzai:** flowcomm, CC BY 2.0 <https://creativecommons.org/licenses/by/2.0>, via Wikimedia Commons
13. **Auroville:** Vyas Abhishek/Shutterstock.com
14. **Science Club:** BNP Design Studio/Shutterstock.com
15. **Composition of Air:** Peter Hermes Furian/Shutterstock.com
16. **Lung Capacity:** inspiring.team/Shutterstock.com

17. **Collection of Late Stone-Age Tools:** Gail Euston-Brown/Shutterstock.com
18. **Bronze Age Objects:** Southern Vadim/Shutterstock.com
19. **Early Iron Age tools:** Sergey Ryzhov/Shutterstock.com
20. **Stack of Magnetic Balls:** MY10/Shutterstock.com
21. **Threads and Yarn:** Neliakott/Shutterstock.com
22. **Marble Balls:** Apostle/Shutterstock.com
23. **Picture of Writer's Daughter:** Credit due to Tania Ghosh
24. **Lost my Keys:** Andrey_Popov/Shutterstock.com
25. **Picnic:** oneinchpunch/Shutterstock.com
26. **Curriculum Vitae:** Kittisophon/Shutterstock.com
27. **Carbon Di Oxide:** Meggi/Shutterstock.com
28. **Water Molecule:** struna/Shutterstock.com